OLDHAM COLLEGE

learning

101 high impact activities to start, end and break up lessons

Dave Keeling Edited by Ian Gilbert

Crown House Publishing Limited
www.crownhouse.co.uk – www.crownhousepublishing.com

First published by

Crown House Publishing Ltd
Crown Buildings, Bancyfelin, Carmarthen,
Wales, SA33 5ND, UK
www.crownhouse.co.uk

and

Crown House Publishing Company LLC
6 Trowbridge Drive, Suite 5, Bethel, CT 06801, USA
www.crownhousepublishing.com

© Dave Keeling 2009

Illustrations © Les Evans 2009

First published 2009.

British Library Cataloguing-in-Publication Data
A catalogue entry for this book is available
from the British Library.

ISBN 978-184590134-9
LCCN 2008936799

Printed and bound in the UK by
Gomer Press, Llandysul, Ceredigion

To the five women in my life* who have all contributed hugely to my ongoing quest for love, laughter and learning.

*So there is no argument, I mean:
my wife Kate, my daughters Rosie and Daisy, my mother Anthea and my mother-in-law, Sandy.

Contents

Contents

Acknowledgements

I would like to take this opportunity to thank everyone for not having this idea before me.

I'd also like to thank all the friends, students, parents and teachers who have sat in classrooms, school halls or conference centres over the years for constantly fuelling my desire to enlighten, empower and entertain. Without them none of this book would be possible.

I hope that reading this book is perhaps the first risk on a long and exciting road to many more risk-taking adventures.

Foreword

You're not having fun, you're using positive emotions to access the limbic system to optimise dopamine secretion to facilitate autonomic learning.

I first wrote those lines in *The Big Book of Independent Thinking* for the introduction to a chapter on neuroscience from our resident paediatric neurobiologist Dr Currran and nowhere are they more relevant than in this book from David Keeling.

We know that the state that the learner is in – their breathing, their emotions, their muscular tension, their entire neurochemistry – will decide how well they will learn. No matter what whistles and bells you add to your repertoire if their state is wrong then the learning won't stick.

However, get the state right and they can't do anything but learn.

Rocket Up Your Class (not our preferred title as the more astute amongst you may have worked out but there are laws in this country. Then again if you can have a whole series of books based around the word 'buggers'...) is a book whose entire purpose is to help you get your learners in the right state for learning. It does so in a number of ways that the simplicity and silliness of the some of the games belies but can be summed up in one word – dopamine.

Dopamine is a key learning chemical that is generated in our heads as a result of a reward or the anticipation of a reward. In other words, doing something we like doing or knowing we are about to something we enjoy doing. Apart from making us feel more switched on and happier this amazing substance is also a key memory chemical. A release of dopamine helps us remember the events of about ten minutes or so prior to the release. The brain likes doing what it likes doing (it is argued that we are genetically programmed to seek out pleasure as it improves our immune system and the more we laugh the longer we live) so when we encounter something rewarding it is in the brain's interest to remember clearly what it was that led up to this pleasurable, survival-enhancing state. So that dopamine rush actually improves our memory for the rest of the lesson. In other words, that seemingly silly game in the middle of the lesson actually works to improve our memory of the entire lesson.

What's more – and this is where the real magic comes in – because dopamine is triggered from the anticipation of a reward, just by coming into your classroom, the place where the good things happen, you start to get their dopamine flowing.

What's more, it is argued that the adolescent brain needs higher levels of dopamine than adult brains so, in a classroom, those year tens are going to get their dopamine either with your help or behind your back. You choose ...

As with all brain-altering substances, dopamine needs to be used in moderation and one long, dopamine-filled lesson will be exhausting to you, them and the senior management team on behaviour duty so you must use these rockets with care and moderation. When you do, you will be amazed at how you will win the trust, goodwill and improve the work ethic in your learners.

So, go on, stick a rocket up your class and see the results in terms of learning.

Ian Gilbert
Santiago de Chile, February 2009

Introduction

Welcome one and all to a *Rocket Up Your Class*, a book designed purely as the intellectual equivalent of a 'firework up the arse' for any lesson.

Whether you're looking for a creative opening, energising middle or big finish to a lesson, then just pick out a relevant game, exercise or idea from this little book of mini-rockets and watch the sparks fly.

Failing that, just leave the room as you found it and head for your local hostelry where Dawn will be waiting with a patient ear, a packet of crisps and your usual.

All the ideas contained within this book have come together over ten years of experience, working the length and breadth of the country with thousands of students in hundreds of schools.

Some of the rockets are of my own devising, some have been donated and the rest have been simply nicked under the user-friendly title of 'knowledge sharing'. But all have been deployed with two things in mind, which are to shamelessly entertain whilst at the same time engage young people in the creative arena in order to prove, as the Greek philosopher Socrates once stated, 'Life and learning should be a festival of the mind'.

Unfortunately, for the majority of people this statement simply isn't true in relation to their days at school.

Put your hand up now if your school experience was a FESTIVAL OF THE MIND!!!!!?

Perhaps a small garden fete of the mind!!!?

Or maybe a wet camping holiday for two of the mind?

If you did raise your hand to the first question, you were either lucky enough to get into Hogwarts or you don't get out enough; either way it's a hugely uncommon response.

I, like the majority of people I meet, did not have a festival of the mind during my school experience. I had fleeting moments but, like many others, I was waiting for someone to create the festival for me.

Every day I would enter the gates waiting for the school to inspire me, for the teachers to entertain me, and when they didn't, I was very quick to point the finger and say:

- School's boring!
- Teachers are rubbish!
- Lessons are c**p!

I took no responsibility for my education whatsoever.

So now my role as a Stand Up Educationalist is to empower and enable young people to take action, and therefore take control of their learning, so that they may leave education having already begun to explore and develop the skills required not just to cope with the 21st century but also to be happy and successful within it.

With that in mind, let the festival commence!!

For each activity, game or idea, I will suggest where I think it will best complement a lesson and explain in what way it will advance the students' experience.

Picture the scene. It's Monday morning, first lesson. It's raining outside and you've got bottom set maths for an hour and all you have for company and support is a lukewarm Pot Noodle and a lesson plan hastily written on the back of a Post-it.

You have three choices:

1 Run

2 Eat the Pot Noodle and run

3 Plough on regardless

Or you could dip into your copy of this book and start your lesson with a quick game of *Thumb Wars*, *Anagrammer* or chuck in a *Thought Grenade*.

You may wish to break it up with an all-out round of *Bagsnatcher* or make it unforgettable with *Quizzical* and *Pass the Exam*.

Or end it with *School Disco*, *Homework Lottery* or *Strictly Write Quickly*.

Whatever the session, whatever the mood, there's a mini-rocket to suit any lesson, anytime, anywhere, that will get the creative juices flowing and engage even the most reluctant pupil/teacher.

So here we go with 101 ways to start, end or break up a lesson, and where best to begin but at the beginning.

The Rockets

1 Smile and Say Hello

When – Every day, every lesson.

Why – You'd be surprised how many teachers don't employ this simplest of tools.

Students will only engage in an environment where they feel understood and then, in turn, more confident (for more info see Dr Andrew Curran's *The Little Book of Big Stuff About the Brain*). This is the starting point for the foundation of a respectful working relationship.

How – Practice in the mirror. Think of someone you dislike being arrested or watch *Shrek 3*. Just don't be miserable because, like gravy and ice cream, miserable and teaching don't mix well.

② Have a Drink

When – When no one's looking.

Where – Stationery cupboard, back of sports hall or in your car at lunchtime.

Why – Why not?

③ Get Naked (I went to a small school in the country)

Only joking. I just thought I'd get the three most popular exercises out of the way first.

You have to admit it though, with these three options you've got yourself one hell of a lesson right there.

Name Game

When – Beginning of term or whenever you may encounter a new class.

Why – It's a quick and entertaining way for you and the students to get to know names and interesting titbits about one another. It breaks the ice and helps to promote a team feel early on, as well as being a superb stand-alone memory technique.

How – The group stands in a circle. The leader (in most cases you) starts off by saying their first name and something they really love.

For instance, *'My name is Dave and I love to wear women's clothing'* (I don't; it is simply an example).

The next person to my left must then say my name and what I love followed by their own name and something they love.

There's a lovely moment in this exercise when it suddenly dawns on everyone that the last person in the circle will not only have to remember everyone's names but also what they love.

You'd be surprised how many people panic at this notion yet haven't realised that by the time it gets round to them it will have been repeated many times over and wired itself deep into their synaptic connections, making their recall magnificent.

You can split them into two smaller groups if you feel the group is too large.

It doesn't just have to be about names. You may wish to focus this memory activity around facts, dates or moments in history.

The key is in the repetition and so for that reason you may wish to read this passage again.

5   Anagrammer

When – Beginning.

Why – In my experience, I've found many times over that if you don't give students something to do as soon as they enter the space, they will almost certainly *find* something to do, like chatting, fighting, groping and not necessarily in that order.

The Rockets

If an *Anagrammer* is up on the board as soon as they enter, it can quickly become a competition with a prize for the longest or most creative or most surreal sentence that can be conjured up in the time given.

This exercise helps the students get into an open and focused state, enabling them to engage more quickly and more effectively within the learning environment.

How – Place a long, scrambled list of letters on the board. The challenge is to find as many words within the list and then create a strange, surreal, cheeky or really long sentence. Letters can only be used once unless they appear more than once.

Below is an example of some letters I randomly scribbled down:

I M O S R A P L D E C T I E D B S

Here is what I came up with:

I PEEL ODD SCABS

I'm sure you'll agree that my first attempt is bordering on genius and that very soon a gold star or Jelly Baby will be winging its way to my door, post-haste.

A lot of joy can be had from this game and you'll be constantly surprised, nay, shocked by the sentences that will spill forth from the mouths of babes.

⑥ If That's the Answer, What's the Question?

When – Usually at the beginning but is just as effective when utilised to break up a session.

Why – I was first introduced to this idea by my friend and colleague Ian Gilbert, celebrated educationalist, lanky sailor and long-time employer (but maybe not for that long). I have also witnessed this exercise being deployed to superb comic effect on the BBC show *Mock the Week*. It is simply a brilliant way to switch students' minds into the possibilities of creative thinking, especially as there is no right or wrong. What a perfect way to draw students to a point of focus, especially if they've just arrived from break where they narrowly avoided a mugging or a deadleg.

How – The answer should already be on the board, patiently waiting to be unleashed at any given moment.

Answers like ... *Only once but it hurt!*

So if that's the answer maybe the question was:

Have you ever tried thinking?
Have you ever tried to kiss a girl without asking?
Have you ever tried to Immac your face?

If the answer was... *Three biscuits and a fox!*

Then maybe the question to this could be:

How do you catch a badger with a sweet-tooth?

You get the picture.

It's amazing to find out how differently the students' minds work and much hilarity normally ensues.

Once the students get the hang of the exercise it can be repeated time and time again.

7 What a Difference a Day Makes

When – Beginning, middle or end.

Why – Revision is not an option and anything that helps the process is a bonus. This is just a quick way to review and revise as you go along. The more you review, the stronger the synaptic connections in our brains become.

How – Give the students two minutes to discuss with each other three learning points from the day before (or five if you really want to stretch them).

Their answers can then be fed back to the class.

 Lesson Trailer

When – End.

Why – To facilitate dopamine release. (Dopamine is a naturally occurring neurochemical that is released in anticipation of, or on receipt of, a reward. It improves motivation and also memory.) Once again, it helps to strengthen the synapses in the brain and, by setting things up for the next lesson, creates excitement and curiosity, both vital for a Festival of the Mind.

How – You can be as creative and as technical as you want. You may wish to record the trailer onto tape or CD beforehand, but for the simplest, live effect, play some tense, exciting music, preferably with no lyrics (may I suggest the opening track to *Mission Impossible* or *Jurassic Park*). Get a microphone, ask the students to close their eyes and then hit them with something like the following in your best American accent.

> 'Coming soon.
> A long time ago in a Russia far far away ...
> He was a man on the edge.
> A mystic, visionary, healer, a prophet whose journey would take him into a world of the supernatural.
> A man shrouded in secrecy, who inhabited a world where temptation would cause chaos.
> A world where rituals and repentance would collide.
> Many would seek him out.
> Many would want him dead.
> Rasputin.
> He's mad, bad and dangerous to know.
> Cert 15.
> Coming to a classroom near you on Monday.
> Check timetable for details.'

Now tell me what self-respecting student would not want to check out *that* lesson?

This technique could become a regular fixture, something the students look forward to hearing, just to find out how good/bad the next lesson is going to be. The more preposterous the trailer the more excited the group.

Stop/Go

When – Beginning, middle or end.

Why – The main purpose of this game is to have fun with a whole-brain thinking approach (using both left and right hemisphere at the same time). It also demonstrates how fixed thinking can severely limit our capacity for transformation and change.

How – I have a confession. This is without a shadow of a doubt my favourite game of all time, for two reasons:

1   I don't have to do it.

2   There is something very amusing about watching a room full of people completely lose all sense of coordination and behave in a bizarre, confused and downright

disturbing way. I hope I haven't put you off.

Ask everybody in the room to stand up; explain to them that there are two rules to this game:

1   No talking unless you suggest it.

2   To do as you ask.

When you say 'Go', they should walk on the spot briskly and with gay abandon. When you shout 'Stop' they must stop immediately as if their life depended on it.

At this juncture you can shout, 'Stop' or 'Go' as many times and in any order as you see fit, just to make sure everyone is singing from the same song sheet.

Now explain that since they have all found this so easy, you are now going to mix it up a bit: from now on, when you say 'Stop' it means 'Go' and when you say 'Go' it means 'Stop'. The faster you say this, the funnier and more confusing it is.

Check for understanding. If there isn't any, say the sentence again but even more quickly.

You can then begin once more and this time just enjoy being witness to a room full of people struggling away with this simple reversal of instruction.

Now it is time to hit the group with some more orders.

From now on when you say 'Clap' you would like everyone in the room to clap once and together. When you say 'Jump' you would like everyone to do a little jump, nothing ridiculous, just enough to see the room move.

Practise this a few times and, quick as a flash, at least 99% of the room will have forgotten the Stop/Go instruction and the fact it's still reversed. Drop this back in and you'll catch out the whole room.

Continue with Stop/Go and Clap/Jump for a minute or two and then get everyone to stop by calling 'Go'.

Confused yet? It gets worse, but it is much easier to play than explain.

From now on when you say 'Go' you mean 'Stop' and when you say 'Stop' you mean 'Go', when you say 'Clap' you mean 'Jump' and when you say 'Jump' you mean 'Clap'.

This announcement will usually be met with looks of bewilderment and utter confusion mixed with screams and a lot of giggling.

You can see the pattern forming. As the leader, you can really let rip by adding to the melee different patterns and then change them using your voice, intonation and dramatic pauses.

To cause even more confusion, create lots more instructions to follow, such as Sit Down/ Stand Up, or Left Arm/Right Arm. The more the merrier.

So get going, or maybe that should be get stopping. Oh I don't know any more ...

10   Tom and Jerry (or Cat and Mouse)

When – Beginning, middle or end.

Why – Fast and furious game which is much more tactical than you might think. It requires quite a bit of concentration, focus, speed of thought and tactical awareness.

How – You will need a decent-sized space for this game to work.

Get the group to pair up. Each pair should find a space within the room and link arms.

Choose one of the pairs to be Tom and Jerry (costumes may help for character motivation). This pair does not link arms.

Explain that Tom must now chase down and capture Jerry. To do this, all Tom has to do is tag Jerry. Once Jerry has been tagged he then becomes Tom.

But Jerry can always tag Tom back so, to get safe, Tom must link on to the nearest pair. As soon as he does so, the person on the other side of the link instantly becomes active in the game and is now Jerry and must be hunted down with stealth and cunning.

The whole room can be used and the other pairs act as convenient obstacles to hide behind.

The game can continue as long as you want or until everyone is running around because nobody knows who Jerry is any longer. When it's firing on all cylinders the interchanges really are quite intricate and complex.

The best way to understand *Tom and Jerry* is to play it a couple of times so that everyone gets the gist.

That's all folks!!

1 1   Thumb Wars

When – I usually play this at the beginning as a warm-up but I feel it can be used any time to raise energy.

Why – To raise energy, I just said that, I wish you'd pay attention. Oh, and it also helps to re-fire the brain. It promotes the use of whole-brain thinking, combining physical, mental and emotional development – not to mention that it's also great fun ... and you get to hold hands.

How – Get the students to pair up and using their right hands (they can of course use their left, if they so desire it) the students must only clasp the fingers together leaving the thumb able to stand up.

Now, like any good game it starts off with a chant and the chant goes like this:

'One, two, three, four, I declare thumb war.'

As you say this, your thumb must move from left to right in time to the chant. If you have done this correctly your thumb will have moved eight times.

If you have done this incorrectly your partner will have got bored and everyone else in the room will be wondering why you can't play a game designed for 7-year-olds.

After the chant, both thumbs must now bow and then briefly kiss, but try not to take it any further. I do not want to be seen openly encouraging inappropriate thumb love.

After this quick bit of pomp and circumstance the object of the game is then to wrestle your opponent's thumb until you have pinned them down in some kind of dextrous half nelson.

The winner is the person who can hold the other's thumb down for more than three seconds.

For a quick competition, my recommendation is best of three.

To raise the game from just a group of people with sweaty hands trying to thumb each other to death into something a little more epic, may I suggest the use of some magnificent music, like *Star Wars* or *Superman*, as this will ensure maximum effect.

You can find *Star Wars*, *The Superman Theme* and other rousing classics on *Dad's Anthems*, possibly the greatest double album since *Now That's What I Call Music 7*.

12 Mucking Furds in a Wuddle

When – Beginning, middle or end.

Why – This is a game of speed and wordsmanship which again activates both the left and right brain as well as helping to widen the group's vocabulary.

How – This can be done alone or in groups.

The object is simply to see how many different words can be made. The letters can only be used once per word (and if you want to really stretch them you could say that they must contain the central letter from the collection). There can be no plurals or proper names.

I would allow a couple of minutes to do this in order to crank up the tension.

At the end you may wish to give a prize to the team with the most words.

This game is often found lurking in the back of papers or puzzle books so there is no problem in finding an endless supply of material.

Have a go now at the one I've prepared below.

Go on I dare you, double dare you, physical challenge ...

D C T

M A U

E P G

Finding just one word is sub-human, ten is mediocre, 30 or more is so good that if people find out they may start to call you names behind your back or leave sarcastic messages on your answer machine in a vain attempt to belittle your mini-triumph. I got 33 and at the time of writing this I am on my own and have seven messages.

For your delectation here are the words I came up with in three minutes (but the easy way, without worrying about the central letter rule. It's been a long day ...).

Cat, pat, mat, eat, peat, meat, tame, came, get, pea, pact, dam, dame, put, pet, met, damp, camp, temp, gut, age, paced, aged, ape, aped, dug, peg, tag, tad, pad, pace, cad, taupe ...

Impressed, eh?

13   Magic Tricks

When – Usually when you really need to pull it out of the bag, not a rabbit but something big, something to make everyone sit up and shut up. I usually use it as an ice-breaker before I begin a session, to find out a few names and to generate an air of curiosity about what, if anything, may happen next.

Why – 99% of students that I meet love to see a bit of magic. Whenever I've said to a group *"Would you like to see a trick"*, they've always said yes. Nobody has ever replied *'No, so stick your rabbit where the sun don't shine!'* (well not yet anyway). Even the most reluctant of students give in when there's literally, and metaphorically, a bit of magic on the cards.

It's still the best way I know to create a curious air to proceedings and add a 'wow' factor.

How – Magic can take years to master and perfect but it's worth remembering that four tricks performed with panache are worth much more than a hundred tricks done badly.

So first of all you need to arm yourself with a deck of cards and a copy of *Card Magic* by Nicolas Eihorn and head straight for the chapter entitled 'Self Working Card Tricks'. These are tricks that require no sleight of hand, rabbits or twins.

They never fail and will never let you down as long as you adhere to the system, and they are the best way to gain confidence in this new and mystical arena. My favourite trick consists of me flicking through a pack of cards (which are face down) and being able to stop at any point through the flicking motion and name the card. It is a trick that never fails to astonish and yet took me all of 30 minutes to master. Now, due to the magicians' code of secrecy it would be wrong of me to print the finer details of the sleight of hand here, but if you purchase the book mentioned above you, too, will soon be able to mystify even the most cynical student. Failing that, send me a cheque for fifty quid and I'll blab the trick down the phone to you without so much as a piff, paff, puff.

Only ever show the trick off to a group when you are sure of it and yourself. I don't know about you, but I'd prefer to be remembered as a Houdini rather than a Pasquale.

14   Tea and Biscuits

When – Once a term.

Why – Why not, it won't kill you, it's civilised, it's British and who doesn't like a dunk when confronted with a task.

I know for a fact that the enjoyment of a full-day staff INSET is directly proportional to the quality and quantity of the biscuits and pastries on offer. So why not do it for the students; they'll love you for it and it's a treat they won't be expecting. They'll be thinking, if you've laid on tea and biscuits, what next?

Pamper day
Free bar
Family holiday

How – If I need to explain this then the world must be coming to an end and there is no hope.

But may I suggest that you can't go wrong with PG Tips and Hob Nobs.

15 Thought Grenades/Thunks®

When – Whenever you like, really, but beginning or middle would be my advice.

Why – A *Thought Grenade/Thunk* is an idea developed by Ian Gilbert (see his book, *The Little Book of Thunks*). Thunk is the term given to the noise your brain makes when it's asked a question when there isn't necessarily a specific answer, just endless possibilities.

These questions were originally designed to promote philosophical thinking in young people but I have found them to be useful in encouraging creative thoughts in everyone I've worked with.

I have even witnessed people radically change a strong fixed opinion based on the thoughts, ideas and comments from other participants.

How – Remember there is no right or wrong, just ideas.

It is the facilitator's job to probe these thoughts and challenge them to see what else may come up.

Here is a selection of 'Thunks'. Some are of my own making and others are from *The Little Book of Thunks*. Feel free to try them out on your friends, colleagues, students or just people you really hate.

All have been tried out on students, and a couple of their answers are in brackets.

1   Can you touch the wind? (No, but you can smell it)

2   What colour is Monday? (Beige)

3   Would Friday be jealous if Saturday went off with Sunday?

4   Is six scared of seven?

5   If a cat could speak what accent would it have?

6   If I stick a bunch of flowers in a computer does the computer become a vase?

7   Can a sheet of red paper be blank?

8   Are most people good or bad?

9   Where does the sky start?

10 Does your nose smell more than your bum?

16 Paper Aeroplanes

When – Beginning, middle or end.

Why – To encourage students to communicate their thoughts, feelings, ideas, and immediate responses to subjects, words or quotes that may appear on the aeroplane.

In a rapidly changing world it's imperative that students develop a voice with which they can express an opinion.

Educationalist Dr Paul Black concluded from his studies of classroom environments that 80% of the questions asked in a classroom are answered by 20% of the students. It's the same few kids!!

This technique works on a hands-free policy (i.e. no hands up) and assumes that *everyone* has a contribution to make – they just might not know it yet. It creates a uniquely random selection process based on the fact that you never quite know where the plane may land.

For this very reason you may wish to keep all windows closed so as to avoid hitting innocent passers-by on the head. (This has just given me a great idea for another exercise.)

How – Again this is open to artistic interpretation. You may wish to conceal within your expertly crafted fighter jet an actual page from a newspaper with a relevant headline, picture or topic. Or you could simply use a blank sheet of paper on which you've added a word, phrase or quote. For instance you could you could write on your A4 sheet a word such as:

Success
Change
Recycling
Learning
Celebrity

Or quotes such as:

'Attitude determines altitude.'
'Make your hobby your job and you'll never have to work again.'
'There is no try, only do' –Yoda

Or perhaps print up a particularly vivid image which directly connects to the theme of the lesson.

Next, fold the sheet into a paper aeroplane and throw it in the direction of the students. Whoever catches the plane – or is hit by it if they're dozing off – has to respond with a thought, feeling, question or statement in response to whatever is contained within the papery folds.

It could be a picture of a young person wearing a hood. You can then ask the student how they feel about the picture. What do they think the 'Hoodie' is like as a person? Where do they live? What do they like doing? How does the media portray young people dressed in this way? Do they know anyone who dresses like this? Do they dress like this? How does it make them feel? How do they think it makes others feel? Should we judge people based on their appearance?

You could also have a picture of the American flag, money, space, a soldier, a school.

Anything as long as it promotes debate.

The questions can go on for as long as you like and can at any point be opened up to the whole class for debate.

17 'In the Style of ...' Themed Readings

When – Beginning, middle or end.

Why – The reading of extracts, I'm sure you'll agree, can be a dry affair. To create a more fun-filled experience, yourself or the students should read aloud under a given theme. This will help to develop confidence and quick/ creative thinking, helping to lift the reading from the norm.

How – In preparation for the lesson pick an extract to be read out and think of a suitable theme, something that will adapt to the style or accent with ease.

Themes such as:

1　The news

2　Kids TV

3　A horror film

4　Superheroes

5　The most confident person in the world

6　A different accent

7　Angry person

8　Someone who thinks everything is funny

9　The most boring person in the world

10　The biggest flirt

You may wish to give an example just to get the ball rolling, so the students get the gist.

As a warm-up try doing the tongue twister below in a Birmingham accent, then try it again in the style of a newsreader or the world's biggest flirt.

> *'I am a thistle sifter,*
> *I have a sieve of sifted thistles,*
> *And a sieve of unsifted thistles,*
> *Because I am a thistle sifter.'*

18 Pass the Exam

When – Middle or end.

Why – Any time around exams can be stressful and this is simply a way to lighten the mood whilst still getting the revision done. It's a memorable exercise and if you wish to add in a bit of choccie, it will help release those little endorphins and that all-important dopamine that will get everyone coming over all excited and remembering.

Music will also help to embed the information being passed around, so think carefully about your choice of music (for more see Nina Jackson's chapter in *The Big Book of Independent Thinking*).

How – I'm sure you must have played this game at some point in your life and if you haven't, then you must have been living in a cave, and a pretty boring one at that.

As with the traditional Pass the Parcel, you must secrete a relevant question, unfinished quote or sum in each of the layers to challenge the student who receives it as the music stops.

If you like the class you may, as I've suggested earlier, add a treat to each layer. If you don't like the class you may wish to booby-trap each layer with perhaps pencil shavings or rubber spiders.

As the controller of music, it is entirely up to you where the parcel stops. Huge enjoyment can be gleaned with the manipulation of expectation and increasing tension as the students await the parcel's imminent arrival.

19   School Disco

When – Beginning, middle or end.

Why – Fartlek, or interval training, has proven to be imperative in the creation of a productive and effective classroom.

Essentially, *School Disco* is a tremendous way to get everybody up and moving, thus increasing oxygen supply to the brain. This not only re-fires the brain but will also aid concentration and energy levels and bring a sense of mischief to any lesson. Plus, from what I've witnessed, most students need as much dance practice as possible.

How – *School Disco* works like this:

At the beginning of the lesson announce that at certain points during the session you will play some music.

Personally, in the past, whenever I thought the room needed a jolt I would blast out the first few bars of 'YMCA'. (This track always gets the party going.) The first table up and busting some classic disco moves receives ten points or a prize.

The table with the most points at the end of the lesson gets to leave the classroom first. If you decide to keep the competition going throughout the academic year, then the team with the most points at the end of term wins a prize, which you may decide is either as amazing as a Ferrari or as disappointing as fudge.

Whatever you decide, this is a great technique that always gets the desired reaction of shock and joy – and what teacher wouldn't want that result every now and again.

20 Homework Lottery

When – Play at beginning, draw at end.

Why – Every student would love the idea of getting out of homework.

So why not make a virtue out of it? Having a lottery such as this will guarantee that you have full attendance every lesson, because no kid would want to miss out on the opportunity of a night off. It will help to create a buzz and excitement around the lesson, not to mention that the money accrued over time can be used to pay for an end-of-term party.

How – You will need a pot and a book of raffle tickets.

Each student, or those that want to, puts their name (or even 20p if you're in that sort of school) in the pot and takes a raffle ticket.

At the end of the lesson the teacher draws out a ticket. The winner, just for that night, is let off from doing their homework. At least this way you know that there's going to be one student who loves your work. (And if you are in that sort of school, you've just raised some money for the PTA cheese and wine evening.)

21 Student Exchange

When – Beginning, middle or end.

Why – To help in the development of the students' approach to teamwork, communication skills and confidence with others and to re-enforce the idea that the person they are now working with may not be their best friend, but they will still have many things in common. Lets face it, even in the working world we sometimes have to work with people whose company we may not enjoy, but this shouldn't mean that we can't still have a productive working relationship.

How – Explain that the students have two minutes to sit with someone they don't normally sit with and then find out at least three things that they have in common.

When the task is complete, the pairs then quickly feed back their findings. It is then up to your good self whether the students remain where they are for the rest of the session or return from whence they came.

Desk Jockey

When – Beginning.

Why – To motivate the students and help them to consider what kind of music may fire them up, relax them or aid their concentration. This exercise also introduces students to many differing styles of music.

After all, music is one of the fastest ways to change the mood of a room, closely followed by balloon animals and swearing.

How – Before the lesson, prime a student on the style of music required – i.e. is it to fire them up or to calm them down? Then allow the student to pick a relevant piece of music to play next lesson.

Do not be alarmed if the music chosen is one you have never heard of and be quick to cover any gratuitous swearing by repeatedly shouting phrases such as Shabba, Com'on, Break it down, Shammo and Stop ... Hammer time!!

23 Teach Us Something We Don't Know

When – End.

Why – Sometimes it's refreshing to let the students know that you are more than just a teacher and that you do indeed have a life outside the science block, or that being a PE teacher consists of more than just blowing whistles and picking on the lazy kids.

It's important to bring a bit of outside inside, to let them see you being human and openly embracing the life of a learner. (Go on, you know you want to.)

How – I envisage this being like the last item on the news, you know, the 'And finally ...' bit where the granny is stuck up a tree or a skateboarding cat brings down a mugger and is given a medal.

Whatever you do should have an element of surprise.

I regularly pass on recipes for quiche and cheesecake, magic tips, strange faces, juggling or anything of interest.

You may wish, with some gentle coaxing, to unleash your prowess with Lego, first aid, electronics, puppetry, driving or stamp collecting (actually, keep that last one to yourself).

So go on, teach 'em something they don't know!!

24   Class Clown

When – Beginning, middle or end.

Why – Wherever I've gone on my travels, there has always been a kid desperate to tell me a gag, and seeing that humour is at the heart of everything that I am and do, I say, give these kids a platform to shine.

It's great fun and can be something the others look forward to, and I guarantee that after a couple of outings this will become a competition, you know, something like *Gag Factor* or *Strictly Tickle Me Quickly*.

How – You may wish to designate an area which will henceforth be known as Clown Centre. It's from here that the mirth will begin. You may even wish to create a hat or costume for a more theatrical feel. If it's the same kid all the time, you may want to ask him or her to research and come up with some topical material.

And just to get those comedy juices flowing, as they say on *Blue Peter*, here's one I prepared earlier:

Q: How many head teachers does it take to change a lightbulb?

A: None 'coz they don't do change. (Boom, boom shake, shake the room.)

25   Smart Arse

When – Beginning, middle or end.

Why – This is more of a technique than an exercise, but I thought I'd include it as it's served me well over the years and we've come so far together in such a short space of time.

Very often, when questioned, students will reply with a grunt or 'I dunno' or 'My dad's bigger than your dad'.

This technique encourages the students to put themselves into someone else's mind and to think outside their usual frame of reference, allowing them to entertain differing possibilities and thus contribute when they didn't know they had a contribution to make.

How – The next time a student says 'I dunno', simply respond by asking this beautifully composed retort: 'Well, if you did know, what would you say?'

If you receive a favoured response, you may wish to celebrate this small breakthrough by uttering the words 'Smart arse'.

26   The Secret of Success

When – Beginning.

Why – This is a quick and brilliant way to see how successful your class is going to be during the lesson.

As I said in the Introduction, many students are waiting for someone to get them energised, open, focused and in the right state to learn. Essentially, they are far too comfortable for their own good.

So much of what's taught in schools is missed because the students are blatantly not in the correct frame of mind to learn anything.

This exercise is used by Japanese *Kabuki* theatre actors as a way of getting into flow or a state of readiness to be awesome. It also develops a sense of personal responsibility and the beginnings of that all-important idea as championed by the Ancient Greeks: 'To know thyself'. In other words, to recognise how you feel and then have the energy to take action and, if necessary, correct it.

The Secret of Success is tremendous fun because it contains two vital ingredients that any student craves:

1   Audience participation.

2   Shouting out.

What could possibly go wrong?

This activity also provides a common language which can then be used quickly and effectively to bring students in line.

How – Explain that you would like to find out how successful the lesson is going to be and that you have an ancient and secret way with which to do this.

Then write down on the board the following words.

Energy
Openness
Focus

At this point it's worth reiterating that this is a game and that they are allowed to smile and enjoy themselves. If this doesn't work then please proceed with exercise 3 and hope no one comes in.

What happens next is this: on the count of three, everyone in the room must shout out a number between one and ten to indicate how much energy they have at this moment in time.

One is a low energy and ten is a high energy.

You will then take the average score and write it down next to the word 'Energy'.

You may now repeat the process for 'Openness' and 'Focus' until you have a score for each one. When this is done, add them up and get the students to work out the total score as a percentage. You may end up with something that looks like this:

Energy – 8
Openness – 6
Focus – 4
Total – 18/30

This immediately helps you with your lesson plan because it's clear for all to see that energy is good, openness isn't too bad, but focus may need some attention. So you know what requires attention before you begin the lesson.

You also have an opportunity to encourage the students to do something about their own energy, openness and focus.

If they're feeling under-energised, allow them to stretch, have a glass of water or massage the person next to them (they might make a friend for life). See excercise 32.

If they are not feeling particularly open, encourage them to sit forward and imagine they could learn something new, and if they are not focused, you have my permission to hit them. Failing that, please see focus exercises 41 or 42.

I have used this exercise 99% of the time in my career and without fail it has helped/ entertained the students into a better frame of mind for the rest of the session.

I'd go as far as to say it's a classic.

27   Giants, Wizards and Dwarfs

When – Beginning, middle or end.

Why – A fun, problem-solving energiser that links into leadership, teamwork, interpersonal skills and contains everything you need for a visual, auditory and kinaesthetic experience.

How – The great thing about this game is the more the merrier. The largest game I have ever played consisted of about 200 students and felt more like a re-enactment of *Braveheart* than a cheeky little livener.

In its simplest form it's Stones, Paper, Scissors, but with a bit of imagination it can feel like you are pitting your wits in a battle of life or death (very much like some lessons).

To play, you require two teams of no less than four a side.

The teams must be facing one another in a horizontal line.

More fun can be extracted if you enlist the help of individual team members to stand like a giant and then make the noise of a giant. Everyone else must now copy this brilliantly realised interpretation of an unnaturally large beast.

Follow the same procedure for the wizard and dwarf.

Once the stance and sound of the characters has been established the teams must huddle together and decide which they would most like to be.

For instance, team A may wish to be giants, team B may wish to be dwarfs.

The next step requires the teams to line up facing each other, about two feet apart.

On the count of three, both teams 'do' their chosen character at each other.

Now here's the important bit that, if it were a film would have tense, repetitive music underscoring it.

Giants kill wizards.
Wizards kill dwarfs.
Dwarfs kill giants.

When the teams first display their characters, what normally follows can only be described as indiscriminate screaming and sheer panic, but after a couple of goes, people quickly get the gist and settle into a more recognised flappy giggle.

Remember that team A were giants and team B were dwarfs, so on this occasion team B would then have to tag as many members as possible of team A (because dwarfs kill giants) before team A can get to a designated place of safety, which is usually the wall behind them.

Whoever is tagged must then join the opposing side. When this happens the game can then be repeated.

The winner is the team with the most players at the end of the allotted time.

The game is tremendous fun and never fails to entertain.

It's surprisingly competitive and you'll know instantly if the group is thinking synchronistically and works well as a team, because more often than not they will pick the same character, thus creating a stalemate.

There's nothing like a bit of creative fantasy to kick-start a Monday morn, or indeed your personal life.

28   I Love You

When – End.

Why – One of the most important and reassuring comments I have ever heard in my life is 'You learn with your heart first, then your head'. I believe that, deep down, we all want to hear those three little words and it works wonders for self-esteem and endorphin release.

I finish all my sessions with these three little words and it's well funny just looking out for the reaction this comment can elicit.

How – At the end of the session, as everyone leaves, just say 'Love you' to each and every one of the students.

Three things will happen.

1   People will smile (may even turn red).

2   People will laugh.

3   You may be surprised how many people say it back!

The title of my contribution to the *Big Book of Independent Thinking* was 'Love, Laugh and Learn'. I still believe it's the best way to embrace life, and in that order.

29   Twenty Seconds to Comply

When – Beginning, mostly, but can be effective at other times.

Why – Sometimes you just get that day or class when everyone seems distracted, unfocused and generally not with the programme.

This system works extremely well because it communicates to the students that you recognise the state they are in, respect it and are allowing them a moment to put it right. This helps in achieving a perfect learning state of respect and understanding, which in turn leads to greater confidence in a learning environment.

How – Quickly explain that the students have 20 seconds to comply and get whatever it is out of their system – i.e. speak to a friend, toilet trip, turn phone off, send a text, etc.

This really does help to achieve a hassle-free beginning when there are those who are hell-bent on fidgeting, chatting or generally making a nuisance of themselves.

You may wish to enforce the 20 seconds by playing the theme music from *Countdown* (just in case you're accused of having a special teacher watch, which passes the time too quickly).

𝟛𝟘   Pub Quiz

When – This may take up a chunk of time. If not, then it may come as a reward at the end of a session.

Why – The vast majority of people love a pub quiz (don't you?). It's fun and competitive and you get to drink, and eat nibbles, and have team names, and never win, and everything.

Revision doesn't have to mean sitting on your own, wishing you were somewhere else.

It can be brilliant if we as educators are prepared to take a few more risks.

I guarantee this is a lesson they won't forget – and for all the right reasons.

How – You will need squash drink, cups, nibbles, bowls, paper, pencils, a CD player, and for a really authentic feel, a microphone. Please be as creative as you want.

You may just want to reel off a set of questions, or you may want to create particular rounds such as:

People/Places
Entertainment
Science
Feel the object
Music
Watch a clip then ask questions

Or whatever you want, as long there's a prize worth fighting for at the end, and for the duration of the quiz it never feels like you're in school.

31   A Bit of Bully

When – Beginning, middle or end.

Why – If it's good enough for Jim Bowen of a Sunday teatime, it's good enough for our education system.

This really is the perfect way to mix up a lesson and add an element of unpredictability to the proceedings.

It also allows the students to feel like they have a major part in how the lesson pans out.

For the dart thrower, it will improve hand–eye coordination.

For the non-dart thrower, it will encourage quick thought and challenge them in a variety of ways.

How – You will, of course, need a dartboard.

May I suggest a child-friendly, Velcro-style board (unless you are a very keen first-aider).

You should divvy up the board into whatever sections you think may benefit the group and create a diverse and interesting lesson. In the time it takes the board to revolve, have a look (page 55) at one version of what your board may look like.

You may wish to change the sections to suit a particular lesson:

Games
People
Spelling
Ten mins to work
Special task

If at any point a student gets an arrow in the 'bull', then it's either a video or all go home.

32 Massage (Feel a Friend)

When – Anytime, but I like to use it in the middle or if I feel the students have been sitting for too long.

Why – We should all rub each other more often (did I really just say that?!).

Massage works, you know it and I know it, so let's not argue.

Not only does it increase blood flow, and thus more oxygen, around the body, it is also a good way of getting rid of tension, both for the giver and receiver (did I really just say that too? Please ignore the ramblings of an idiot and just 'Carry on Learning').

This is a fantastic way to look at trust, teamwork and confidence and is an exceptionally fast way to have a giggle and re-energise the room.

How – Ask everyone to stand. If possible, get them to stand in a circle, if not then they can stay at their desks.

Ask the students to turn to their right and massage the person in front of them, then stand back as you are met with a cacophony of 'Errrr', 'Aaaaaghhhs', 'No way', 'Get off' and other defensive mechanisms, but they soon get the hang of it.

You may want to suggest some chopping hands and also remind them to massage above the waist only.

After this shout *'Stop, turn to your left and now it's payback time!'*

This is when the massaged becomes the massager.

I suggest you just enjoy the show. The energy will go through the roof, just like the teacher next door 'coz it sounds like you're having a lot more fun than they are.

33   While We Are On the Subject

When – Beginning or end.

Why – During my time in education I have been lucky enough to work with some extraordinary people who have proved to be inspiring in many ways. I have also been privy to some great advice, the following being one of the best:

The Rockets

The biggest learner at home should be the parent. The biggest learner in the classroom should be the teacher.

A lot of teachers have explained to me, very close up and with much gusto, that there simply isn't enough time to learn anything new.

Well, now there is.

This is a technique/challenge to keep you sharp.

How – Challenge the students to come up with a question relating to people, places, things, then your job is to go off and find the answer or as much info as you can before next lesson.

This are not only good for your general knowledge but shows clearly that you are happy to engage in the learning process too.

Here are a couple of testers to see if you are up to the task in hand:

1   What does the acronym SCUBA stand for?

2   What sports were represented at the very first Olympic games?

3   What is the strongest animal in the world?

4   Where does the word 'grey' come from?

5   What is the name of the ginger gene that gives me my very distinct pigmentation?

If you wish to do this during the lesson you can use the latest text phenomenon called AQA (Any Question Answered). Just type in any question and text it to 63336 and an answer will be despatched to you very quickly indeed. Some of the answers are hysterical. And all for £1!

Good luck and may the farce be with you always.

34 Should I Stay or Should I Go?

When – Beginning or end.

Why – It is so important for students to think about themselves and their skills, and to reflect regularly on their contribution to the establishment that we commonly know as school.

The world of work will continually test them in this way, so it's vital that they are encouraged to look at themselves as part of a group, and recognise that in a world full of change those that develop, adapt, reflect and take action will prosper.

How – Ask an individual or group to come up with three great reasons why the school should allow them to stay.

This can be as long or as short as you want, depending on the time you spend debriefing the answers.

In the interests of research you may wish to ask yourself the very same question right now. The answers may surprise you.

35　Ringing or Minging

When – Throughout.

Why – All my work within education is based on the four principles contained within the mnemonic R.I.N.G.

Relevent
Interesting
Naughty
Giggle

If these four elements are taking place within a lesson, then you will have a creative and unforgettable learning experience, and surely that is what every educationalist seeks on a daily basis.

If you have one of those elements taking place, you'll remember it. If on the other hand you have all four, you will never forget it.

When students readily see the point of a lesson – if the content is interesting and the curiosity quota is fulfilled, if it's cheeky or challenging, and if it's a laugh – then not only will their confidence soar, but they will want to return to the lesson and that, my friends, is a power shift worth nurturing.

 How – Each and every activity in this book.

36 Sleep (but never call it that: call it 'The Art of Relaxation')

When – Beginning or after a vigorous activity.

Why – Regardless of all the wonderful and creative learning techniques that are out there for us to make full use of, ultimately the students will have to sit down and take a test. This will require them not only to be able to control their nerves but also the ability to get themselves into enough of a relaxed state to be able to access all the information contained within their walnutty noggin (or brain if you want to get technical).

Relaxation allows the blood to flow and thus oxygenate the brain, which in turn allows the freedom to access information already stored within the brain, or indeed allow in new information.

Relaxation also helps prevent the 'reptilian' response mechanism which goes into operation whenever we feel anxious, stressed out, fearful or threatened. Our brain, in this situation, shuts down and goes into survival mode, which basically means we use very little of its potential for learning.

Being relaxed can allow us to bypass this response and engage more of our brain's potential to spark up. Not to mention the fact that students love it if you suggest a quick cosmic sleep.

How – The students should sit in their chairs, bums to the back of the chair with feet flat on the floor about a hip width apart.

The spine should be at the back (if it's not, seek medical advice) and should be as straight as possible. I like to imagine a metal pole sticking out of the top of my head, pulling me up and slightly forward (you may also have strange voices telling you to do bizarre things).

Once the students are sitting correctly you can then get them to concentrate on their breathing: using deep breaths, breathing in through the nose for the count of four and out through the mouth for the count of four.

Doing this and only this for between two and four minutes will, with practice, enable the students to emerge calm, cool and collected.

If anyone emerges a little giddy or really tired, they are probably not used to breathing so deeply, but these feelings will diminish with practice.

While the students are in this relaxed state of mind, you may wish to ask them to visualise a goal or to think about where they are in terms of their confidence or school work and what they are doing. Is it working, and if not, what could they do to make it better.

If during this exercise somebody actually falls asleep, then they were either exceptionally tired or you are in fact a very powerful wizard.

37   Twenty Questions

When – Beginning.

Why – It's a classic game and a really good opener in terms of focusing a group and allowing them to work at their questioning skills and ability to work together to achieve a common goal.

How – Decide on the object and let the questioning begin. If for instance it is your go and you choose 'sausage' it is then up to the rest of the group to discover your sausage by asking only 'Yes' and 'No' questions. Questions such as:

Is it big?
Can you eat it?
Does it have moving parts?

As the title suggests, allow up to 20 questions per go and then ask the students to guess what they think it is.

A visible scorecard may be useful in terms of generating a competitive element.

 ## History Repeating

When – Beginning or end.

Why – I truly believe that to evolve effectively, we must develop our ability to reflect on what we are doing or, in this case, what we are not doing.

Students that do this quickly recognise that they have the facility to change moment-to-moment, day-to-day, as long as they want to.

It starts now.

How – Prepare the students by asking them to think about something they didn't do yesterday that they are going to do today.

For instance, here are a couple of responses that I have had in the past:

1   Homework

2   Contribute more in class

3   Turn up (and that was a teacher)

4   Bring a pen (we all have to start somewhere)

This is not rocket science but if done regularly even these simple things contribute to making a more effective and switched-on student.

39   Poet's Corner

When – End.

Why – Rhyme, rhythm and music have proven to be incredibly important in the creation of high impact and long-lasting learning, which is why when I say to you:

Hickory Dickory Dock.

You can't help but reply:

The mouse ran up the clock.

Exactly! Now you don't set your alarm clock for 6 o'clock every morning just in case a gangly ginger bloke one day asks you if you know the words to a classic children's nursery rhyme. You simply went over the tune enough times in the playground until it was so hard-wired into your brain that you couldn't forget it if you tried.

That, my esteemed colleagues, is what memory really is. It's little and often (and maybe some other really intricate things that are far too complicated and neurological to put in here).

What a quick poem or limerick or ditty can do is generate a fun soundbite which contains all the facts and is easy to recall, especially when under the pressure of exams.

 How – The best way to approach a little ditty is to have a go. Start small and then build up. It may start as a couple of lines and end up an epic.

And so to recap this exercise I have just penned this gentle reminder:

At the end of the lesson, turn to your class,
And announce that you have an extraordinary task,
That within five mins they'll produce a rhyme,
One that is useful and finished on time.
A jingle which recounts the important stuff,
The bits you forget and always fluff!!
So to avoid this pain and constant derision,
Compose a poem called 'Ode to Revision'.

Caption Competition

When – At the beginning, to be judged at the end, or a fun note to end on.

Why – An easy but effective way to start a lesson and get those young minds ticking in a proper fashion.

The more pertinent the picture is to the lesson the better, as it will fix their minds on the topic of the day.

It is a really enjoyable task that I swear will create much mirth.

How – Check out these pictures below and see what captions you can come up with.

41 The Gallery

When – End.

Why – Revision is still not an option.

Sometimes we all need a push to be more creative in our revision. This exercise, very much like *Poet's Corner*, is a fast, fun and brilliant way to draw all the key components of a lesson together and cement them in our heads. It is highly visual and the results can be mounted on the wall, thus keeping a record of all the work.

How – With five minutes to go, set the challenge.

'You now have five minutes to draw a picture that recaps the main lesson points or sums up the lesson. It can be literal, abstract, stick figures, cartoonesque, mind map/spider diagram. The more doodly the better.'

To create a more nostalgic and reflective art-inspired mood you may wish to play the gallery music from *Vision On* whilst the students stand back to admire each other's masterpieces.

42   Yes/No

When – Beginning, middle or end.

Why – Another classic, this game is like the stocking filler of games. It works anytime, anyplace, anywhere, with anyone. Never failing to entertain, this game is very effective in quick thinking and fast questioning which, when coupled with the ability to stay focused under pressure, really sorts out the men from the boys, or indeed the ladies from the lasses.

How – You need two volunteers.

One will ask the questions, the other is not allowed to answer with the words 'Yes' or 'No'.

The person who lasts the longest time whilst adhering to these rules is the winner.

Are you ready to play?

If your answer to the last question was 'Yes' or 'No' then you are out already and should be ashamed of yourself for falling into the oldest trap imaginable. Remember, you are to set the highest example at all times.

Do you understand?

You've done it again!!

This game may be well beyond your understanding, in which case you should begin with a relaxed game of Snap and build up from there.

 Ball Game

When – Beginning or middle.

Why – The ball game is very effective in the development of teamwork and the art of communication and is an exercise I have used many times throughout my career. It very cleverly demonstrates when teams are, or are not, working well together.

When it works it is fluid and almost magical.

When it fails (which it does often) it's simply a right bloody mess, with balls dropping here, there and everywhere.

How – You may require a bit of space for this one, so a quick bit of cardiovascular exercise and 'Hey presto!' all the chairs and tables have moved to the sides. I normally challenge some of the lads by betting them a quid that they can't clear away the furniture in less than two minutes. They always achieve it and I am satisfied that it is a quid well spent.

The next step is to get the students to stand in a circle, along with yourself.

You are now going to establish a throwing pattern which will stay exactly the same throughout the game.

You will be first to throw the ball. To do this you need to make eye contact with someone across the space, say their name and then throw them the ball. The person with the ball then repeats the process and so on and so forth until everyone in the circle has received the ball once and has thrown the ball once.

Repeat this same pattern with one ball several times to really imbed the throwing sequence.

Remind everyone at this juncture that they only have to concentrate on two things to make this game work.

1   Who you throw to.

2   Who throws to you.

Everything else is just a distraction.

You may wish to add more balls once you feel the students are comfortable with the game. My current record is eight balls all moving around rhythmically like one entity. It really is quite breathtaking when everyone is working to make the game a success.

When more balls are added you will find that the game will quickly dissipate into chaos and mayhem as people panic, throw the ball too hard, don't say their partner's name before they throw it or aren't focusing because they're laughing so hard at someone who has just been hit in the head.

This will continue to happen until the students learn, through practice, to focus solely on the two objectives mentioned earlier.

And remember, it is not the size of the balls that matters but what you do with them ...

 ## Countdown Conundrum

When – Beginning or middle.

Why – This exercise is magnificent for focusing the group. Not only does it provoke intuitive responses but it also teaches students the ability to listen and feel comfortable with silence and resist the urge to fill it with rubbish.

When this works it is almost eerie – as there is no order to it, it just happens.

How – Get the students into a circle if you can, or just let them sit where they are.

Explain that the objective is to count from 1 to 20 but that nobody knows who is going to say which numbers, they are simply to say the next number in the sequence when it feels right.

If two people say the same number at the same time, you go back to 1 and start again.

The students could have their eyes closed during the game in order to help them really listen and tune in to the group.

If you go back to 1 a lot of times, the group may get frustrated. As the facilitator it is your job to get them to relax and focus on the job in hand by letting it happen. There are no extra points for completing the game quickly.

If you do eventually mange to count to 100, then you must have entered a higher state of consciousness and from now on shall be referred to as God.

45 Anyone Who

When – Beginning, middle or end.

Why – This is a high impact game that plugs right into the curiosity centre of those taking part.

It allows the students the freedom to ask searching questions of themselves in order to find out more about the group. It also requires an open-hearted approach and the ability to be truthful.

How – Students must be seated in a circle, with one person standing in the middle. That person's objective is to ask the group a question that is true of themselves, such as:

1   Anyone been to Disneyland?

2   Anyone ever been bitten by a horse?

3   Anyone ever called their teacher 'Mum'?

Anyone sitting in the circle who answers 'Yes' must immediately vacate their chair with the speed and agility of a gazelle and sit in another empty chair within the circle. The person who asked the question from the middle has to try to grab a seat and sit down.

If at the end of a go you're the one finding yourself alone, in the middle wondering where it all went wrong, it means it is now your turn to ask a question of the group, and so the game continues. The rules are: you can't just move to the chair next to you because that is downright lazy, and you can't return to your own seat.

The more probing you can be with the questions, the more fun can be had.

If you're really clever, you can think of questions that will guarantee that everyone has to move.

Approaching this game with 100% conviction will ensure its place as one of the top three energisers of all time.

Fruit Bowl

When – Beginning or middle.

Why – *Fruit Bowl* is a quick, enjoyable energy raiser and a sure-fire winner with anyone who has ever been denied the opportunity to shout 'banana' at the top of their lungs during morning lesson.

How – Students should be seated on chairs in a circle.

Your job is then to walk around the circle and allocate each person with a fruit that they must remember: orange, apple, banana, orange, apple, banana and so forth.

If the person in the middle shouts 'banana', then everyone who was named a banana must immediately leave their chair and sit in another vacated chair within the circle.

If the person who shouted 'banana' manages to sit down during the melee, a new person will be left in the middle, and so the game continues until everyone is sweating and has developed an inner hatred for any fruit-based comestible.

Oh, it may be worth adding at this point that if the person in the middle shouts out 'Fruit Bowl!' then *everybody* in the circle has to move. This is normally when all hell breaks loose and you have a trifling panic on your hands.

The rules are very similar to the game *Anyone Who*.

You can't just move to the seat either side of you nor can you just run back to your own seat.

You can change the fruits to suit the mood when the group becomes more confident. May I suggest, through experience, and for comedy value, the fruits listed below:

Plums
Melons
Kumquats

You may think it immature and silly, whereas
I think it memorable and very funny.

I dare you to see who is right.

Dictionary Corner

When – Beginning or end.

Why – This is a lovely way to enthuse
students with a curiosity and love of words
and so help with vocabulary and
communication.

How – Randomly select a word in the
dictionary and explain the meaning. It is then
the students' job to memorise the word and
then use it at least three times during the
day.

It's not always as easy as you think. Since
writing the last entry, I have used the word

'betwixt' twice today, and only yesterday had to insert the word 'nonclemature' whilst ordering fish and chips which was, in itself, a moment of sheer genius.

 Future Interview

When – End.

Why – This exercise looks at the power of visualisation and is, if you like, a rehearsal for future success. The exercise gets the students to imagine the most successful future they could have, where everything has gone to plan, and it then encourages them to describe how they did it.

By doing this, the students are actually advising themselves on what attitude to have in order to achieve their goals and what action to take next.

Future Interview can be very powerful in re-enforcing the messages of goal setting, networks of support and attitude in the world of work.

The Rockets

How - Divide the group into pairs. Allow the students a few minutes to imagine that they are 25 years old and are exactly where they want to be in terms of their family, friends and career.

Now explain that because they have been so successful, Jonathan Ross would like to interview them on his show to discuss their life and achievements (and then ring their granddad and leave a rude message).

The pairs must now decide who is A and who is B. A will pretend to be Jonathan Ross and will interview B first. If there is an odd number, the students may take it in turns to be interviewer/interviewee. At this point you can unveil the five questions that you would like A to ask B.

1   Where are you now? (i.e. at the age of 25, not geographically)

2   How did you become so happy and successful?

3   Who helped you get there?

4   When did you take responsibility for your life?

5   What advice would you give to young people who are watching and who dream of becoming successful and happy like yourself?

My advice would be to put these questions on a board or flipchart so that everyone can see them at all times.

When A has interviewed B, then B can interview A. The person being interviewed must give as much detail as possible. When everybody has finished it is a good idea to bring all participants back together for a debrief and to find out what their answers to the questions were.

Take as long as is needed for this exercise. You can add an air of tension and excitement by counting down to a live transmission. You may even want to play a bit of chat show music.

49   Hot Gossip

When – Beginning or end.

Why – I don't know about you, but I love to know what's going on. I am a curious little being. In terms of developing relationships and emotional intelligence, it is imperative as an educationalist that you have a foot in both camps. In my experience, all the best teachers make it their business to know what's going on.

Simple questions such as:

The Rockets

1   Who went out last night/and what did you do?

2   Did you see the football/*X Factor*/*Hollyoaks* over the weekend and what did you think of it?

3   Who's going out with whom?

4   Who's got the latest (insert name of coolest group you've heard of) album?

5   What did you have for your tea last night?

You'd be amazed where some of these questions can take you. As an educationalist, it also gives me some common ground which I can come back to time and time again. It may mean that just by asking the questions above I now know that George loves his food, Laura thinks she's got the X factor, Paul goes out with three girls a week, and Alan wears eyeliner and thinks he's a rock god – and I haven't even left the staffroom!!

See how much you can find out next lesson. Before you know it, you'll have an incredibly detailed group profile and a greater understanding of what makes the group tick.

How – Ask!!

Take a general interest!!
Have some fun with it!!
And more importantly, trade info!!

50 Supercalifragilisticexpiallygoogle

When – End.

Why – This is a challenge to see how good students are at collecting evidence and digging up information.

It allows them to engage actively with a vast resource (T'internet) and extract the finest material. This is a skill that will become increasingly handy throughout their life in the 21st century.

Not to mention that the more bizarre the request, the more enjoyable the quest.

How – Suggest it; search it; learn it.

Here's a few things you may like to supercalifragilisticexpiallygoogle.

1 Inventions (modern)

2 People called Brian

3 Crisps (most bizarre flavour)

4 Local history

5 Yourself (if you haven't already)

51   Globetrotter

When – End.

Why – A lot of students that I work with haven't even ventured out of their immediate town. In the 21st century, with the world becoming much smaller, it is vital that young people have a greater understanding of the world which they inhabit. *Globetrotter* has been created to do just that–to give students an interest and knowledge of the world around them.

How – You will need a spinning globe (see Argos cat no. 267/1097 for more details).

Choose a student and ask them to close their eyes, spin the globe and stop it with a finger: they will then have to find three or five interesting facts relating to that country, which they will then feed back at the next lesson. Other students should feel free to add any other relevant titbits of information.

That's it! As simple as that. Before long, the class will have built up a good knowledge of where places are and what may be happening within them.

So buckle up and have a good trip.

Rock 'n' Rolla

When – Beginning, middle or end.

Why – To add a bit of risk to a lesson why not plan the whole thing with the roll of a dice.

Now before your eyes roll back into your head and you start to have palpitations, with a bit of planning you'll still be fully in control of a lesson which is seemingly delivered through chance.

When I have done this in the past it has proven to be challenging, risky, rewarding and utterly unforgettable.

How – All you need is a dice – the bigger the better. Decide beforehand what each number on the dice may represent. For instance:

1   Play music

2   Watch a film

3   Play game

4   Work in silence

5   Discussion

6   Make something/go practical

You can also prepare the exercises beforehand, so you will be much better primed for any eventuality.

It will appear to the students that the whole lesson was created from moment-to-moment, with as good a chance of watching a film as working for ten minutes.

If the class is behind in their work, you may like to weight the dice in your favour so that the work gets done (but just in case anyone asks, you didn't hear that from me, alright?).

So roll up and roll away, everyone's a winner.

I'm a Celebrity Get Me Teaching Here

When – Beginning.

Why – It's tricky being creative all the time and putting yourself under unnecessary pressure to come up with the goods for every session. Well, this is a technique that I have used consistently with teachers and is a very speedy means to brainstorm in a way that will take you outside your frame of reference. And seeing as you have a ready-made audience of quick, inventive minds, it would be a shame not to utilise it fully.

Not to mention that, with this exercise, students are given the opportunity to explore the generation of ideas, concepts and problem-solving *and* will unwittingly assist you in the formulation of future lesson plans.

How – Tell the class to pick a well-known face, maybe a celebrity or preferably somebody who is 'current' and with whom the students identify, then simply ask the congregation to imagine and discuss how that particular person would conduct the lesson. What unique skills, qualities and ideas could they bring to the proceedings?

If it was David Beckham for instance (for some reason he comes up a lot) he may choose to set the classroom up in a four, four, two formation, with oranges and drinkies brought out at half-time.

Instead of telling off a student for talking or mucking about, you may wish to issue a system of yellow and then red cards if it's for blatant misconduct.

He would probably insist on a pre-match chat to fire up the team and to encourage constant communication, so everyone knows what everyone else is doing, perhaps working in pairs or threes (football's favoured triangle).

You can see already that many ideas will spring forth quickly using *I'm a Celebrity Get Me Teaching Here*. Many of these can then be used to keep up interest, focus and curiosity quotas, and all just by imagining your lesson from someone else's perspective.

Below are some other people/characters that you may like to investigate and put to the teaching test:

1 Shakespeare

2 Madonna

3 Peter Kay

4 Homer Simpson

5 Simon Cowell

Story Makers

When – Beginning or middle.

Why – This is an exercise that first came to my attention whilst working with Independent Thinking associate Mike Brearley (see *Emotional Intelligence in the Classroom* for more of the charming Mr Brearley). Storytelling is at the heart of communication and emotional intelligence and has been so ever since human beings had the good fortune to interact. We all have a story to tell and have all benefited, grown up, developed and been educated through story-telling. Not only does this exercise help with the communication of thoughts, feelings and ideas, it also – and, I feel, more importantly – assists in the students' ability to listen, and listen properly.

Listening is the most underrated form of communicating, and in a world full of collaboration and constant change it really is a skill we could all benefit from tuning in to.

When was the last time you felt you were really listened to?

How – Split the class into pairs. One is now A and the other B.

A's job is to tell B a story of a time in their life when they felt genuinely scared. All B has to do is listen properly. To do this B must first make regular eye contact and more importantly must resist the temptation to butt in, ask questions, add their own take and generally take over (this is much harder than you think).

When the A pair have completed their story, B must now repeat it back to A, and this time with A doing the listening.

The whole process shouldn't take more than ten minutes.

There will be a variety of responses to this exercise. Some will really enjoy being listened to; it will make them feel important and confident. Some will feel a little uncomfortable with this new level of intimacy; even eye contact can be a challenge for some.

Interestingly, a lot of people, when they hear their story back, are surprised at how non-scary it now appears, coming from someone else, and they will begin to wonder what all the fuss was about.

For me, the beauty of this exercise lies in its simplicity.

It is so rewarding to watch people's reactions when they are allowed to engage in an open and honest way. This goes a long way to creating a solid team who are much more at ease and aware of each other and their stories.

Everyone has a story. Some are completely gripped by their story and seem incapable of changing it so their past dictates their future and becomes a self-fulfilling prophecy. Others know their story, understand it and can effectively transform it through action and change.

Do you have a story?

Or does it have you?

55   Get Knotted

When – Beginning or middle.

Why – An excellent exercise to illustrate team-work and also for the value of patience, communication and bendiness (stay with me).

By creating a human knot, the students will have to combine working together, problem solving and the ability to look ahead – if they ever wish to get untangled and be home in time for tea.

How – Arrange the class into a circle and ask them to stretch out their right hand and grab the right hand of someone opposite them; they can then do the same with their left hand, making sure that they always grasp the hand of somebody opposite. There must be at least two people between the two.

Once everybody is connected, the game can begin. It is imperative that once the connections are made they cannot be broken, either to further the progress of the group or for a sweaty hand break.

It will be obvious to all those taking part that they are now in an almighty tangle, a complex knot of Gordian proportions, if you please. The objective now is to get out of the mess and back into a circle as fast as you can without breaking the chain.

This may sound impossible and I must admit I always thought it was, too, until I was part of a team of insurance salespeople who managed it. Heady days ...

So if a ginger bloke from the East Midlands and a group of middle-aged office workers from Bournemouth can do it, so can you!!

56 Up 'n' Under

When – Beginning, middle or end.

Why – A superb energiser which is great for concentration, hand/eye coordination, group morale and is competitive as hell.

How – I was reminded of this game when I saw a group of women doing it with water

The Rockets

balloons when camping on a hen weekend (don't ask).

You need two teams of no less than five.

I prefer to use a balloon rather than a ball or a beanbag because I like the end to go with a bang.

The teams must line up alongside each other about two feet apart.

The person at the front is the captain and will be holding a balloon.

On the word 'Go!' the captain must pass the balloon between their legs for the person behind to retrieve, they then in turn pass the balloon over their head to the person behind who then passes it between their legs, and so the game continues.

When the person at the back receives the inflated air bag of joy they must run from the back to the front and pass the balloon between their legs and so on and so forth.

The winning team is the side whose captain has passed right through the team and has run back to the front and sat down on the balloon, popping it.

If the balloon doesn't burst, then you lose.

So up, up and away with your beautiful balloons.

57   Liar, Liar, Knickers on Fire

When – Beginning or end.

Why – This game looks at quick thinking, communication, confidence, body language, and is a current favourite of mine.

How – Divide the group into two teams.

Each team then needs to pick three people who are going to play. When the lucky three have been chosen they decide on a story which is only true for one of them.

The three then make their way to the front of the class and tell their story.

It could be similar to the example below which I recently heard whilst playing the game at a corporate event:

'I once, accidentally, killed a penguin.'

(May I remind you, the reader, that at no point should animals be harmed during this game.)

The volunteers then each tell their own unique version of how this event occurred.

The more realistic, the better. Remember, you don't want the opposing team to guess the right person, otherwise you lose.

After they have all told their version of the story, the opposing team can then ask up to three questions to each of the storytellers. After that they must state who they think is telling the truth.

If they choose the correct truth merchant, they can have either a point or a prize.

If they get it wrong they leave with nothing.

At this point it's the other team's turn to try to pull the wool over everyone's eyes.

You've Been Framed

When – When you most need it or feel the students could do with a lesson off.

You can only ever do this one once!!

Why – Sometimes you just have that session where no matter how creative you are or how good a teacher you are, nothing seems to work. Well, that's where a good laugh and the promise of money can be a great motivator.

So let's make full use of it by encouraging the students to work together in order to generate a classic TV moment you can all enjoy time and time again.

How – You will need a video camera, some creative ideas and someone who doesn't mind falling over a lot (there's always one of them). Oh, and it's also a good idea to have someone who is pretty useful with a video camera. With this group of talent you can't fail.

PS: If you know somebody who has access to a paddling pool and a trampoline, then this is a bonus. You've seen the programme on telly where people send in video clips of themselves falling over and in return get £250. So your challenge, if you choose to accept it, is to stage a moment of school-based slapstick, film it, send it in to ITV and await your cheque. Worst-case scenario, the cheque never arrives but you have a good laugh watching Sammy fall of his chair during a video explaining how dangerous farms are. Best-case scenario, your clip is shown on prime time TV, Sammy gets his own half-hour sitcom and you have enough money to start your own farm.

This exercise really is a one-off, so make the most of it and send me your clips.

Food for Thought

When – Beginning, middle or end.

Why – Okay, so *You've Been Framed* may be too much of a logistical risk for some of you, so here's an exercise that won't be.

It is now well documented, through our knowledge of learning styles, that many kids learn much more effectively when snacking or imbibing in some way. Hence, the water policies that have been introduced in many schools over the past few years.

So why not help create a more conducive learning environment by occasionally putting out a selection of brain-grazing foodstuffs to help release those neuro-related happy chemicals which are a necessity if you want to embed the practice of life-long learning.

You may already be doing something similar, but I felt it was worth adding.

How – Think small buffet or, if you're known in the staffroom as a tight wad, think small plate, enough for one each.

I'm thinking one or a mixture of these:

Fruit
Vegetables
Cheese
Flapjacks
Chocolate (it's not all for you!!)

You may choose, if you haven't already, to have a basket of fruit out all the time, for students to pick from whenever they require a burst of energy. The choice, of course, is yours.

60 Child's Play

When – The whole lesson.

Why – The majority of people I work with in my sessions loved their primary school experience.

We all remember those heady days when we couldn't wait to put our hands up to answer a question or volunteer for something.

So why does that youthful exuberance pack up and move out as soon as we enter the secondary school gates?

Why not take the students back in time and show them what the fuss was all about. Show them that playing is the key to creativity and learning.

How – Explain that, for the purposes of this lesson, the students will need to imagine they are 6 years old.

You may wish to set up an activity on each table so that the students can rotate around when their interest wanes. For instance, there may be water on one table or sand or Lego or paint or a play area or Plasticine. The idea is to allow the students the space and time to discuss, reflect, be creative and explore the themes of the lesson in diverse ways – you could make each activity about teamwork/ problem solving.

One table may have an envelope containing a list of words that the group must make into a sentence and then discuss. The table with sand could be a competition to see who can create the most sandcastles in a minute. There may be a table with paints where the task is to recreate a masterpiece using three colours and the hand you don't write with.

The real crux of this exercise is to have as much fun as you can while at the same time challenging the group in a variety of ways.

Don't forget to have a glass of milk, a biscuit and a quick sing-song half way through.

Review the work through stories, pictures, poems and create a display of the finished articles.

You decide, as long as it's in keeping with the primary school feel.

61   Quizzical (If quizzes are quizzical what are tests ...?)

When – Whenever needed.

Why – An onslaught of information can be pushed in a student's direction during a lesson, and sometimes it can be difficult to decipher what is really important and what is not. Sometimes it helps a great deal if you can separate the 'must-know bits' and create an air of pomp and circumstance around them. This will go a long way in allowing students to absorb the material and effectively recall it.

How – Whenever I meet a new group I will very quickly use the space to my advantage. For instance, I will tell the newly assembled group that I have two rules when I am working.

If I walk over to the left-hand side of the room I'm going to say something *really* important and you must remember it. The stuff in the middle of the room is good but this information on the left is life or death.

To aid their memory I ask them to sit forward, because we have memory in our muscles (see exercise 63), and make a sound that suggests this is, without a shadow of a doubt, the most interesting thing they have ever heard.

This can either be whoops, hollers, ooooohs, aaaaghs, eeerghs, hmmmms or blahhhs, depending on the group.

You may wish to repeat this part for no other reason than comic effect.

I then explain that if I move to the far right it is because I'm angry, frustrated, disappointed or because some people are being disruptive or distracting. But I never get angry because, whatever happens, I still get paid (I hope!!).

I reinforce their confidence by announcing that I won't have to go far right because my expectation is that they will be brilliant (they usually are).

This simple technique allows you to really emphasise where the key learning points are, using the methodology of *Quizzicals* (dangly bits of info!!).

Yes But, No But

When – Beginning or middle.

Why – This quick exercise is not only a bit of a giggle but it also shows very cleverly the power of the 'Yes' as a positive force.

I was reminded of this game having just read *Yes Man* by Danny Wallace, a very funny story about a guy who, for a sustained period of his life, says 'Yes' to everyone and everything – a very funny read and I heartily recommend it.

How – The students get themselves into pairs. One is A, the other is B.

Explain that it is now A's job to ask questions or make suggestions, whilst B's job is to just say 'No'.

This soon becomes frustrating for A because the conversation can never go anywhere; they just keep hitting a wall of negativity.

The next step is for A is to keep making suggestions, such as:

Shall we go out?
Do you like films?

Have you ever seen a grown man naked?

Probably not the last one but you get the point.

This time B replies 'Yes ... but ...' and then comes up with a reason why they shouldn't.

We've all done it, though, haven't we? Remember this one?

Q: Have you done your homework?

A: Yes ... but the dog ate it.

This form of conversation is more infuriating than just saying no because for a small moment it all looks good and then the rug is pulled out from under you.

The final exchange sees A still making suggestions, but this time B has to say 'Yes ... and ...'.

For instance:

A: Shall we go to the cinema?

B: Yes ... and when we get there I'll buy the ice creams.

A: Do you like reading?

B: Yes ... and when I've finished this book you can borrow it.

It is clear for all to see that being more positive and open and resisting the opportunity to block, by saying 'Yes ... and ...', keeps the conversation positive and pushes it on, creating a myriad of different possibilities and opportunities.

It is vital to remind students to remain open-minded and positive within the learning space.

63 Muscle Memory

When – Whenever, but I find towards the end as a recap is useful.

Why – Scientists have discovered that we have memory in our muscles. The majority of us learn best by 'doing': it's like riding a bike, the physical movement helps to spark up the brain into action.

The best thing about this technique is that it's like writing the answers on your body but no one can see them.

How – I was introduced to this exercise by my long-time friend and colleague Roy Leighton, a man whose work has touched us all in some ways and some of us both ways. A man who has been a constant source of inspiration and amusement.

Essentially, you need four things for a great memory:

1   Structure.

2   Emotional engagement (you need to want to do it).

3   Imagination (think ridiculous and try to link it to at least two of your senses).

4   Review a little and often.

Structure is incredibly important when developing a strong memory. It is said that for every seven random things we learn, for every one after that we will forget one, mainly because it is not linked to anything else in our heads.

The beauty of this activity is that we get to use our own bodies as a learning tool.

So the structure is as follows.

First and foremost do the following:

Point to your:

Head
Ear
Nose
Mouth
Shoulder
Down your pants
Between your knees
Feet
Hold out your left hand
Hold out your right hand

With this in place, we will now need ten random objects that you will place around your body. Let us say for argument's sake that the lists of objects looks like this:

1 Car

2 Giraffe

3 Mobile phone

4 Pencil

5 Teddy bear

6 Pterodactyl

7 Spectacles

8 Wig

9 Microwave

10 Caravan

We will now place the objects, one-by-one around the body, using our imagination and senses to create as strong a link as possible.

So, point to your head. What do you have on your head?

You have a car.

Big or small?

What colour? Remember it can be any colour.

Dream make?

What is the car doing? A press-up, singing karaoke, making a trifle?

Once you feel the object has been well established you can move on and repeat the process.

You will be amazed how quickly and effortlessly these objects will become seared into your memory, and I know without a shadow of a doubt that you will never, ever forget you have a pterodactyl down your pants.

You and your students can have a lot of fun with this exercise and it can be useful to memorise all kinds of info from times tables to equations, recipes to world events.

Remember it's not just you and your volunteer out front doing this, it's everyone else in the class as well.

You may now wish to look around and make sure the coast is clear. Non-involved passers-by may become unduly worried if they see you randomly pointing at your body and shouting out objects that don't exist.

Show and Tell
Show but Don't Tell
Tell but Don't Show

 When – Beginning, middle or end.

 Why – A brilliant technique that allows students the chance to express themselves and give others a glimpse into their lives and hobbies.

It is also there to help develop confidence and communication for the 'shower', and ideas, questioning and teamwork skills for the observers.

 How – Brief the students on what is required of them. It may be an unconnected object or it may be linked to a specific topic. For instance, you could ask the students to bring in an objected related to their greatest achievement, or something they have made recently, or something connected to their parents' profession. Basically, anything that will arouse curiosity and allow us, the observer, a sneaky peek into our fellow students' lives.

Then, as the title suggests, you may want the students to eloquently describe and name what it is they have with them.

Or you may wish to add an element of surprise by asking them to describe it without showing it, leaving the audience to guess.

Or you could just show the object and let the audience discover, through a series of cleverly concocted questions, what the connection is.

65 *EastEnders* Moments

When – End.

Why – I wholeheartedly believe that, in order to create a culture of curiosity, excitement and passion, every lesson should end on an *EastEnders* moment.

The BBC uses this technique brilliantly to keep Joe Public coming back time and time again to watch people with mockney accents being miserable.

If it works for the Beeb then it can work for you. Imagine if you were in a science lesson and at the end the teacher said:

The Rockets

'Okay, if you'd like to extinguish your Bunsen burners then I will tell you all the amazing secret of ... Duff, Duff, Duff, Duff, Duff, Duff.'

Kids would be screaming at you desperate to find out *'What is this secret you speak of?'*

Students would be camping outside your classroom cooking beans on a little stove chanting, *"Must find out, must find out!!'*

TV and radio exploit this cliff-hanger mentality to the full to keep their audience engaged, so why shouldn't you.

How – Think about your lesson, the learning outcomes, and how you can leave the class dangling for next time.

It's probably not as hard as you think.

It may even make you want to come back.

If you can't think of an *EastEnders* moment see exercise 8 for ideas.

66 Sponge Ball Square Chair

When – End.

Why – I used to play this game at Cubs as a high-impact, competitive energy raiser. It's incredible how much energy is generated and expounded in such a short space of time.

How – For this game to be really effective you will require a bit of space and a sponge ball (Early Learning Centre is good for this).

Split the room into two teams and then number them off. Team A sits down on one side of the room facing team B who are sat down on the other, like this:

1 2 3 4 5 6 7 8

8 7 6 5 4 3 2 1

Place a chair with its back facing inward at either end of the room. From now on these are the goals.

As you can see from the diagram, the teams are numbered in the opposite direction.

You are now the referee (treat yourself to a whistle, go on, you know you want to).

Your job is to be in charge, call out the numbers and make sure nobody gets hurt (a bit like going on a school trip).

If you shout out 'One', then both number ones have to run as fast as they can into the middle, get the ball with their feet and try to score by kicking the ball through the chairlegs. They then return to their seats when one goal has been scored and another number is shouted out, and so the game continues until everyone is wheezing from the effort and a striplight has been smashed.

To give the game more of a team dynamic, and make it a little trickier, you may like to call out more than one number at a time.

The team with the most goals at the end of the allotted time wins.

I like this game so much that I am now off to force my kids, and anyone unfortunate to be passing my house, into a marathon game of *Sponge Ball Square Chair*.

This, I have no fear, will become a class favourite.

1–10

When – End.

Why – The fastest and best way to sum up a lesson: quick feedback that immediately lets you know if they have understood the lesson and that you are doing your job properly.

How – At the end of the session ask the students to shout out a number between one and ten.

Pick the first number you hear (say it's six). The students then have to create a six-word sentence or just six words that tell you what they have learned, enjoyed and remembered about the lesson.

It really is as simple as that.

Phil Beadle (a former Teacher of the Year and guitar hero from Channel 4's *The Unteachables*) loves this exercise. Do you need any more convincing?

All right, here a few variables on a theme:

Once you have asked for a number, then ask for a letter between A and G.

So for example:

Number 4
Letter B

The class now must come up with four words beginning with the letter B that best sums up the lesson.

So you could end up with:

Brilliant, Blinding, Bodacious, Bonkers.

Just imagine what words you could use if the lesson was a bad one.

This activity really challenges the students to be honest yet economical and creative with their feedback, which, may I add, is a good thing for a busy person such as yourself.

 ## Instant Replay

When – End.

Why – Fast and furious. Recapping a little and often is a tremendous way to have fun with revision and is vital in the development of long-term memory.

How – With five minutes to go, split the room into three groups and explain that in two minutes, and as fast as possible, they must brainstorm everything that has taken place within the lesson.

Next, pick one group (more if you have the time) to come up to the front. They now have two minutes to act out the entire lesson, warts and all, from start to finish.

Always funny, and you'll be amazed at some of the tiniest details that find their way into this monumental performance.

Granny's Footsteps

When – Beginning or end.

Why – Time for another classic from my own childhood which draws on a group's ability to work as a team in order to claim the forbidden treasure (or in this case a bunch of keys).

It also, and very clearly, illustrates that we as a nation are quite useless at standing still.

How – One person is 'granny' and she will stand at the end of the room with a bunch of keys or any other 'treasure' placed directly behind her.

The rest of the group are stationed at the other end of the room, ready to embark on this adventure of a lesson-time.

The objective is to get the keys (or whatever) from granny's end (you know what I mean) to the other end of the room without being detected.

Granny is allowed the chance to turn round at any moment she chooses. If she does use this power, the group must immediately freeze (yes, even their mouths).

If granny sees you move, then you must return to the start. If you are in possession of the keys you must drop them first and then return to the start.

The real crux of this game is to get the team working as a group to trick, distract and befuddle granny so she can't keep track of the keys.

It is with this united front, and ability to silently move as one, that will ultimately be the reason that granny is left both clueless and keyless.

For extra pleasure – use a real granny.

70   Strictly Write Quickly

When – Beginning, middle or end.

Why – A real tasty goal-setting exercise with a touch of Hogwarts thrown in.

It gives the students room to scribe freely their hopes, dreams and aspirations without restraint.

It also shows how much written work can be generated in short, sharp bursts.

How – First, encourage the group to take a couple of minutes to just sit and think about where they would like to be in ten years time, what they would want to be doing, who they'd like to be and how they would like to feel.

Then explain with great awe and wonder that, when you utter today's magic word (I like to use 'floccinaucinihilipilification') the pen or pencil will immediately become a magic one and that anything they write down in the next three minutes will come true in the next ten years.

It is so heartening to see students furiously scribbling down their future successes.

The most interesting discovery with this exercise is that 99% of their magical scrawl is more than achievable without magic.

71   Arrested Development

When – End.

Why – It is always encouraging to see students arguing why a lesson has been a real benefit rather than assume that it is there simply to get in the way of their social life.

Employing a technique such as *Arrested Development* gives students a platform to prove that their education is, in fact, working for them.

How – Put this question to an individual or group:

'If you were arrested for having learned something in this lesson, would there be enough evidence to convict you – yes or no?'

If the answer is 'Yes', I suggest you give them a few minutes to discuss their findings with their peers.

It is now your job to facilitate the onslaught of positive educational affirmation and teaching prowess.

If the answer is 'No', then please see all other exercises for help and guidance.

72 Elevator Pitch

When – End.

Why – Fast, funny and fundamental in assisting students in habitual review.

This activity comes fresh from the world of advertising and enables your captive audience to cut straight to the chase of any lesson.

How – The premise is to be able to sum up the value of the lesson and key learning outcomes in the time it would take a lift to

travel three or four floors, i.e. 10 to 20 seconds.

You may split the groups up to discuss their pitch beforehand or challenge them on the spot.

73 Total Recall

When – End.

Why – You may have noticed that many of the titles used for this book point doggedly towards my undeniable penchant for TV and films of the 1980s. Please do not let my love of wobbly sets, dodgy special effects and corny, pun-filled dialogue put you off your one-person mission to put a banger up the comfy inner sanctum of the educational establishment.

Remember, and to loosely quote an epic sci-fi classic: 'In last lesson no one can hear you scream'.

So with that in mind let us press on.

This game is like a mongrel version of *Elevator Pitch* (excercise 72) and *Just a Minute*. It once again proves that working together means success.

How – Split the room into three groups so that they may prepare their ideas to review the session.

Ask the groups to pick a representative or spokesperson to come to the front.

Their job is to review all aspects of the lesson for as long as they can, without hesitation, deviation or repetition. If they fall foul of any of the above, then they and their entire group are eliminated (from the game, not from life).

The winning orator with the best time, and their respective group, get to leave the class first. The losers leave last.

It is always amazing to see how motivating an early release can be.

74   Flippin' Hell (Coin Tosser)

When – End.

Why – This idea came from Ian Gilbert who probably nicked it from someone else. You know how these things are. It is a real cracker and pushes students to work together and make sure each other is prepared, otherwise both parties could lose out.

How – Students work in pairs and are given 10 to 15 minutes to prepare for a test. When the revision time is up, the students must flip a coin. Whoever loses the toss must now take the test. Now here's the clever sixth sense style twist: whatever the outcome of the test, both students must share the grade.

Evil, isn't it?

75 Heads or Tails

When – Beginning, middle or end.

Why – A group-friendly game that ultimately can give you a quick and seemingly random way to get volunteers.

How – Ask the group to stand. Explain that you will flick a coin. If they think it's going to be heads they place their hands on their heads. If they believe it's going to be tails they must place their hands on their posteriors.

The winners of each round stay standing; the losers sit down.

Very quickly the room will dwindle till you have the number of volunteers you require.

This can be a life-changing exercise.

As a direct result of winning this game at a recent corporate event, I was given the opportunity to lead Birmingham City Football Club out onto their pitch in front of 30,000 screaming fans.

Living the dream!!

76   This Lesson's Rubbish

When – End.

Why – Another variation on the review and revise theme (you can never have too many in my book. Not *this* book, my metaphorical book).

How – Towards the end of the lesson, hand out small bits of paper and ask the students to privately scribble down a keyword or phrase, question or date, i.e. something that relates directly to the topic of the lesson. They then screw up the paper and put it in the specially provided bin.

When all the rubbish has been collected, you can randomly select a piece of discarded challenge and throw it back at any student you like (or dislike for that matter). Their job is to respond with a thought, feeling or statement regarding the subject matter.

When this is done, the students are provided with the opportunity to throw the paper into a different bin, for recycling purposes.

Tidy room, tidy mind.

77   Ministry of Silly Rules

When – Beginning.

Why – To cultivate an air of silliness to accompany everyday structure. To celebrate play and openness in a learning environment.

How – At the beginning, ask five students to each come up with a rule for the lesson. I suggest that you whittle down the rules to three per lesson, using the time-honoured tradition of the clap-o-meter. The louder the clap, the better the idea.

You may get rules like these:

1   All answers must be preceded with the student's own unique buzzer sound.

2   Everyone must get up and swap seats every ten minutes.

3   Every time the teacher turns to face the front, the students must clap.

4   At the end of the lesson every student must shake the teacher's hand and thank them for their time.

5   Every vocal contribution in the class must start with, 'Well, darling, if I may ...'

As long as the rules are not detrimental to anyone's health or well-being, they should be seriously considered.

See what your class comes up with next lesson, and please let me know the funniest suggestions.

78 Mastermind

When – End.

Why – A good chance for the chosen Mastermind to be grilled on several subjects, and a great opportunity for the group to concoct exciting and adventurous quiz questions.

How – Once the Mastermind has been chosen you can split the room into three groups.

The first group must come up with five questions pertaining to the class subject.

The second group must come up with five questions on general knowledge and the last group will stick to the Mastermind's specialist chosen subject.

This game/quiz can be rolled out over the term, so everyone gets a go. Highest score wins.

To add to the tension, you may wish to turn out the lights, position a lamp over the challenger's chair and play the original TV *Mastermind* theme tune.

Go on, you've started, so you may as well finish.

79 Beat the Teacher

When – End.

Why – The draw of this game is that the students get to pit their wits against the teacher. Now what student wouldn't want to mentally destroy their teacher in front of a home crowd?

The questions that the student will face should all be topic-based and so meet the revision brief.

How – The teacher and challenger should sit out front, facing the rest of the class.

The remaining students should be split into two groups.

One group will devise a series of ten modern, culture-based questions for the teacher, while the others will create topic-based questions for the student.

The questions for the teacher and student will be asked in turn.

Whoever gives the most correct answers will become the undisputed champion and should take great pleasure in gloating about their new-found intellectual superiority.

Trip Down Memory Lane

When – End.

Why – A brilliantly realised memory technique that can be applied time and time again and always comes up with the goods.

It also encourages the students to interconnect life and learning.

How – Get your students into a nice relaxed state (see exercise 36 for more details).

Once they're relaxed ask them to visualise their journey to school. Start by leaving the house and along the way pick out ten obvious structures or objects.

For instance:

1   Dad's car

2   Front garden

3   Litter bin

4   Youth club

5   Indian restaurant

6   College

7   Poundstretcher

8   Bus shelter

9   Pub

10 School

Once you have ascertained the structure/visual aids you should now memorise ten random objects and put the technique to the test by linking the objects to your chosen memory trail. Then, to remember them, just walk the trail in your mind's eye.

To give you an idea, if your first random object was a buffalo you could link it to your dad's car by strapping it upside down to the roof rack, or have it drive the car or be changing a wheel (this is all in your imagination, please do not attempt these ideas for real).

You can see what I'm doing, so you can now apply the same method to the other nine objects.

It is as simple and as effective as that. Once you and the students have practised it a few times, you'll find the exercise can be applied to memorise all different kinds of info.

81 Yes Let's

When – Beginning, middle or end.

Why – This game is purely about openness, confidence and embracing the moment. It also celebrates the positive freedom that the word 'Yes!' can generate.

How – Make it clear to those assembled that whenever you suggest an action, such as press-ups, dancing, walking like a monkey, etc. everyone else must respond as positively and as joyously as they can by shouting out 'Yes let's' and then perform the action until someone else in the group comes up with a new action, and so the game continues.

When approached with gusto, this game is at once liberating and exhausting (you try doing squat thrusts continuously whilst waiting for a group of shy kids to come up with another action!!).

82   Change Ends

When – Middle.

Why – Just like half-time in sport or intervals in theatre, it is always beneficial to get together and discuss how the first half of the lesson went. Reflect on the positives and negatives and then look at how, individually and as groups, they can go out and improve the second-half performance. Reflection is the key to self-awareness, and the first step towards positive change.

How – Middle way through the lesson announce half-time (you may want to indicate this by using a whistle or playing music). Next, gather everyone around in a huddle and begin the half-time chat.

By getting the students to suggest how they or the lesson may improve in the second half, they will also have some emotional buy-in to the smooth running of the session and to making it productive and enjoyable, because if they don't, they will in fact be dissing their own advice and ideas.

Clever, huh?

 ## Group Therapy

When – Beginning, middle or end.

Why – Schools that will move forward in the 21st century are the ones in which the students are allowed and openly encouraged to educate one another.

This activity allows the space and time for this process to happen, whilst arming the students with the desire to seek out information and answers for their own gratification.

How – Check for group understanding at any point you see fit.

Ask those who understand the learning point to raise their hands.

Those that haven't got it yet have three minutes to approach a classmate with their hand in the air and get them to explain, as clearly as possible, the ins and outs of this little nugget of info that up till now has eluded them.

84   This is Not a Chair

When – Middle.

Why – This is an improvisation game from my drama school days which focuses on openness, creativity, invention and play.

How – You will need a chair!

Sit the group in a circle with the chair in the middle. From now on only two people may enter the space at any one time.

When they do, the objective is to create a brief scene using the chair as a prop.

It can be anything – a hat, a badge, a parent, a gun – whatever their imagination comes up with. The only thing it can't be is a chair.

As the facilitator it is up to you to keep the game moving along quickly, so when you think one idea has been established, send in another two students to take over as chair deniers.

85 Bag Snatcher

When – Beginning, middle or end.

Why – To develop the students' tactical approach to problem solving, as well as getting them up and moving.

How – This is a more tactical variation of *Sponge Ball Square Chair* (see exercise 66).

The students are set up exactly the same way, except there are no goals at either end, and in the middle of the floor there lies a beanbag, not a ball.

The objective here is to get the beanbag back to your chair. But here's the catch. If you grab the beanbag and are tagged by your opposite number, then you must drop the beanbag where it is and return to your seat.

The game is not just about speed and grabbing the beanbag, oh no, no, no, no.

It becomes much more about patience, waiting for the right moment or opportunity to distract your partner so that you can perform the delicate extraction without being nabbed.

Much more difficult and therefore much more competitive.

Order!! Order!!

When – Beginning, middle or end.

Why – This activity looks at non-verbal communication skills and teamwork. It is successful in focusing groups in a systematic and thoughtful way.

How – It is up to you as the leader to decide what challenges you want to set, but all must be performed in a non-verbal way and must only finish when everyone is in agreement with the end result.

Below are some of my suggestions for challenges you may choose to explore.

1 Get in order of height.

2 Get in order of birthdays.

3 Get in order of hand size.

4 Get in order of hair colour.

5 Get in order of smartest to scruffiest.

Go forth and create order in your classroom.

Crafty Kids

When – Beginning or middle.

Why – I first came across this activity whilst working on a project with the Tate Modern art gallery in London.

This activity rapidly engages the students into a right-brained creative approach to working and concentrates very much on the development of visual/spatial intelligence.

How – Students, where possible, should stand in a circle. Each member needs to be armed with a ball of the finest Plasticine that the Early Learning Centre has to offer.

This doughy ball of dreams should be held behind their backs.

The challenge is to make, mould or craft a model of an elephant (or whatever you decide) out of the Plasticine. The group has two minutes to do this.

A lot of fun can be had with this exercise, coming up with different ideas of subjects to model, maybe a dinosaur or a self-portrait, or you may decide that you want the model to represent something that the students have learned within the lesson; it could be a person, landmark or object.

It is always a good thing to give the students time to peruse each other's handy work, looking for similarities/differences.

This activity proves beyond doubt that we are all inherently creative but more often than not are either seeking permission to be so or do not have a sufficient outlet through which our creative juices can flow.

 1 2 3

 When – Beginning or middle.

 Why – This is a game that beautifully links the left and right sides of the brain and appears very simple but has had many a head teacher flailing about screaming for their mummy.

It is a game which brings the art of listening, communication, rhythm and action together in the form of an Irish jig (stay with it). The activity also clearly shows the brain's response to small changes.

How – Students must be in pairs.

Phase One

The first phase of this game is to get the pairs facing each other, making good eye contact and alternately counting to three.

So, A says 'One', B says 'Two', A says 'Three'.

B says 'One', A says 'Two', B says 'Three' and so on and so forth.

Allow them time to establish a rhythm and seek feedback from the couples as the game progresses. (Normally the students are feeling quite relaxed at this early stage).

Phase Two

Announce that you are now going to make a small change.

The pairs now no longer say 'One' but replace it with a clap of the hands. 'Two' and 'Three' are still vocalised.

Let the group tackle that.

Phase Three

The pairs no longer say 'Two' but instead replace it with a raspberry sound (if you cannot raspberry you should be ashamed of yourself but I will allow a click of the fingers, just this once).

The rhythm should now look like this:

Clap, Raspberry, 'Three'.

Phase Four

The pairs no longer speak at all, with 'Three' now being replaced with a stamp of the foot.

So the jig should now look like this:

Clap, Raspberry, Stamp.

By now you may have noticed that it appears you have a classroom full of spit-sodden, clap-happy, spasm jockeys.

One by one, the students' brains have caved in under the intense pressure of the tiny changes put in place.

Some students, of course, will respond favourably to the actions instead of words, but all will have exercised their whole brain and bodies.

Ten Chairs

When – End.

Why – The *Ten Chair* exercise is a goal-setting staple that wonderfully illustrates how important it is, as success habits guru Stephen

R. Covey once wrote, to 'begin with the end in mind'.

The willing volunteer in this exercise will embark on a ten-year journey beyond sight and sound where they will look long and hard at decisions and choices that they will have to make in order to achieve their hopes and aspirations.

This is at once a powerful and thought-provoking denouement to any lesson which will have a long-lasting effect on all those who take part.

How – You should allow a good 20 minutes for this exercise to be truly worthwhile.

You don't have to use ten chairs exactly. I will leave the number of chairs required to your discretion. I, myself, tend to use seven, to make the point.

Put the chairs out in a row.

Have your volunteer sit in chair one at the start. This chair represents today.

Ask them if they would kindly move to chair ten in the line. This chair now represents ten years into the future.

Get them to visualise where they are in ten years time: what they are doing for a career, where they live, who they are with and how it feels to have acquired their dream job and dream life.

It is essential to this exercise that this visualisation is as positive as it can be.

You then begin to work backwards along the timeline by moving to seat number nine and discussing with the group what needs to be in place and what kinds of things you need to be doing to make it successfully to seat number ten. You then do the same thing with seat number eight and so on ...

Keep moving back until you are seated back in chair one again, i.e. today. Then ask, *'So what is it you need to be doing today to be best prepared for tomorrow, next week, next month, next year, next five years, to end up in ten years time exactly where you want to be?'*

The essence of this exercise is about taking action now and putting all the right steps in place today to secure the exciting future you dream of.

Fascinating when you think that all these feelings can come from what is essentially a line of chewing gum-infested school chairs in a dimly lit classroom.

That is how powerful our imagination can be, and it's why time should always be spent at each chair in the timeline to create the most positive and productive outcomes.

90   Class Act

When – End.

Why – For fun, confidence and the chance to get you and your mates out of class earlier.

How – Split the room into three to five groups.

The groups must decide between them who has the best party piece. The chosen few must come up to the front and in turn perform their quirk, talent or impression.

It is then up to the age-old clap-o-meter to decide who is the class act and who just needs 24-hour care.

The winner and their group will leave the lesson first, as a just reward for their endeavours.

⑨① Scrappy Do

When – Beginning, middle or end.

Why – This game is designed to get the juices of invention flowing and has the luxury of being ever present throughout the lesson, so that students may add to or modify when the moment of divine inspiration takes them.

How – Before the lesson, place a carrier bag or tray on each table.

It should contain anything arty-crafty, such as card, scissors, pipe cleaners, cotton balls, Blu-Tack, stickers, lollipop sticks ...

You can announce that at the end of the lesson a prize will be given to the table that produces the best representation of a famous landmark, person or anything you desire.

You may want to link the arty-craftyness to a theme within the lesson.

Let the building commence!

92   Diary Room

When – End.

Why – It is always useful to record what you've learnt at the end of every session, but students will often just drop what they've done and move immediately on to the next class without so much as a by-your-leave.

This game allows the group space and time to use their own technology to record quickly the lesson outcomes, and helps them build up a live record of their learning, which can always be jotted down at a later date or, indeed, put on a disc as a future revision technique.

How – If you are feeling brave and have the space, you might like to create a little area in your classroom with a couple of cushions or a beanbag with a sign above it that designates it as a *Big Brother*-style Diary Room zone.

All you do from that point onwards is to leave a couple of minutes at the end of each lesson for the students to record onto their mobile phones their thoughts, feelings and key learning points.

Quick, easy and very useful for later on in the year.

Silly Walk Tag

When – Beginning or middle.

Why – An energy-raiser with a difference, this game requires players to multitask by formulating lists whilst running around like headless chickens.

How – You will need an open space for this one. To begin the game, one person is designated the catcher whilst everyone else must place their hands on their thighs and must keep them there for the duration of the game. (Even if they have an itch.)

Their hands can only be released from the upper leg when they are actively attempting to catch a fleeing class member.

When you are caught, you instantaneously become 'on' and your catcher must quickly suggest a topic that you will have to list continually until you catch somebody and suggest a different list for them to name.

For instance, the topic could be flavours of crisps, in which case you would proceed after the gaggle of waddling, work-shy fops whilst shouting 'beef and onion, salt and vinegar, smoky bacon, cracked black pepper and Arabian sea salt' (I shop at Waitrose). Or 'hand-picked, jet-washed, secretly trained, tatty slices, thrice blended in a confused booze infusion and a sprinkling of winky tinkles'.

These aren't just any crisps, these are made up for the purposes of a book crisps!!

You never know, I might get an advert off the back of this.

This game is actually a lot harder and more fun than its name suggests, but you will have endless joy coming up with new and more ridiculous topics for the students to chew on.

Friend or Foe?

When – Beginning or middle.

Why – A game that is all about stalking should never be ignored, especially when it buzzes up any room and generates so much energy and laughter.

How – Again, this is best done in a large space.

Instruct the students to move around the space and in no particular direction.

Explain that whenever you clap your hands they must immediately change direction. (For those of you reading this who love a bit of power, this hand clapping instruction is delicious.)

You can now introduce the main feature. Ask the students to stop moving and, without making it obvious, they must decide on a person in the room whom they love more than life itself (reassure them that this is only pretend). When they are given the cue to start moving again, their job is to keep as close to the person as possible without letting them realise who is stalking them.

Now let's put the cat amongst the pigeons and really mix things up.

Ask the students to stand still. This time ask them to think of someone in the room who is now their enemy, they really don't want to be anywhere near this person and will do whatever they can to keep as far away as possible, whilst still aiming to keep as close to their friend as possible, without being detected.

What happens next is hilarious, as everyone attempts to get close to their friend, who may in fact have chosen them as an enemy.

Confused? You will be. Let down? You won't know until you try it. This game is always funny because of the bizarre relationships that members of the group are bidding to cultivate.

Chicken Run

When – Beginning or middle.

Why – To build confidence, trust and a sense of fearlessness and risk taking.

How – Clear all desks to the side of the room and position the students at one end. At this point it is imperative to explain that this game can only be successful if everyone creates an environment of trust and works together as a group to ensure the safety of others.

Pick a volunteer who must go to the other end of the room.

Instruct them to close their eyes and then, when the moment takes them, they must run down the room towards their classmates, as fast as they can.

Before you collapse with worry, let me explain that in all the years I've been doing this exercise only one student sprinted all the way down the room and hit his classmates at full pelt. No one was hurt because his classmates and I were there to catch him.

What happens 99% of the time is that the runner, out of sheer panic and disorientation, never gets over half way without breaking out into a bizarre and camp little trot, arms flailing at invisible obstacles. What is important is to see if the students can trust in themselves and others and run openly and freely, despite the fact it goes against every fibre of their being.

This is one of those exercises, because of the emotions of fear and excitement involved, that students never forget.

96   I'm a Genius

When – Beginning, middle or end.

Why – According to Thomas L. Friedman's *The World is Flat* the future of employment lies within the realms of possibilities, innovation and creativity.

So, in a bid to start the ball of invention rolling, I was inspired by the Radio 4 panel game *Genius*, hosted by Dave Gorman, which built nicely into a quick game I use with students to see how inventive they are.

How – Prime the students to think about inventions that would change their lives, or other people's, and jot down a quick explanation of what the idea is and what it does.

Pick three students who must come up to the front in turn and read out their inventions.

It is then up to you and the rest of the class, through a debate, to decide whether this idea/invention is 'genius' or not.

If it is genius, then maybe they could receive a special badge or sticker with the word 'Genius' emblazoned upon it.

If not, then they leave with nothing.

Welcome to the fickle world of *Genius*.

97   Success Election

When – End.

Why – *Success Election* looks at confidence, communication and debate and requires students to think about success and the qualities that make up a successful person.

How – Allow students a couple of minutes to think about someone whom they think is successful.

It doesn't have to mean the person has achieved something monumental, but it does have to be someone who has inspired them. They can be young or old, famous or not, alive or dead.

In the past, I have had such luminaries as Homer Simpson, Bill Gates, Wayne Rooney, an auntie, a granddad, a brother, a mother and Spiderman.

It really shouldn't matter who it is; what does matter is that the student has the ability to argue that their candidate is more successful than anybody else's, and how they achieved that success.

Once everyone has chosen a candidate they must then pair up and take it in turns to argue the case why their person is the most successful. The pair must agree on the winner, based strictly on the strength of the argument given.

When this has been achieved, the pair teams up with another pair to create a foursome and they proceed to argue whose representative is now the most successful.

When the group has decided whose person has won out of the two current winners, the foursome can then join another foursome and so on.

This pattern can continue until you have about four or five winners.

When you reach this stage the winners can then be invited to the front, where they in turn will be announced and given time to make their claim for the most successful person.

The overall winner will be decided once again through the ancient art of clapping or screaming or even a secret ballot.

The beauty of this game is that despite the fact that the great and the good are always up there being represented, more often than not it will be an auntie or grandparent that comes through on the outside and takes the title.

And they say you can't choose your family!!

98   Postcards from the Edge

When – End.

Why – Another really useful goal-setting exercise which enables students to write to their future selves. There is something very powerful about committing your goals to paper. It's almost like you're contractually bound to achieve it, especially given the added twist that this contract will at some point in the future be returned to you.

How – Each student is given a postcard. On the front they must write their name and address. On the back they should follow this structure:

The Rockets

I.................. (their name)

Am going to.................. (their objective, which must be specific and measurable, achievable, realistic and time-related).

I will achieve this by.................. (NB This is not the date, but in practical terms, i.e. *how* they are going to do this).

The postcard must now be signed.

Your job will be to assist the students in making the target as specific as possible and to help with creative ways in which to fulfil this short-term vision.

It is entirely up to you when to return the postcards.

I wouldn't actually post them (have you seen the price of stamps these days!?).

I suggest you whack them in a drawer or filing cabinet for safe keeping and return them when the students most need a gentle reminder or physical proof of their achievement.

Key Game

When – Middle or end.

Why – This is a powerful Stanislavskian technique of setting objectives. (Stanislavski was a Russian practitioner of method acting. If you haven't read his works, you must. You get a free ring binder with Part One.)

This exercise has an almost magical quality about it and never fails to draw gasps from bewildered onlookers. After the first go, you will also have a queue of ready and willing operatives, desperate to go do the voodoo that you do so well.

How – Clear a space and gather the students to one side of the room.

Pick a volunteer and explain that you would like them to retrieve a set of keys that you have dropped somewhere on the floor about half way up the room. Once the student has seen you drop the keys they must then be blindfolded. Explain, clearly, that they must now walk purposefully towards where they believe the keys are.

The Rockets

When the student feels the keys are right in front of them they must bend down and pick them up. What they can't do, but will attempt to do, is to shuffle across the floor using their feet, like some sort of primitive metal detector, hoping that they will kick the keys. This behaviour is not allowed.

What will happen is this – the student will almost always fall short of the keys and miss them entirely. It is very rare, if ever, that anyone goes beyond the keys.

The next phase works like this:

You take the student back to their starting position and explain that you would now like them to focus solely on a chair that you have placed at the other end of the room. Their task is again to walk purposefully down the room to the chair. When they feel the chair is right in front of them they must turn around and sit down in the chair.

It is worth repeating this instruction to make sure the student is clear and focused on the task in hand.

You may then blindfold them.

Give them a moment to adjust to the blindness and mentally focus on the chair and their objective.

Explain that when they're ready they may proceed (and here's the genius bit) but, on the way, could they pick up the keys, which you immediately drop about half way up the room.

This is where the magic takes place. More often than not the student will stride forward, bend down, pick up the keys and move on towards the chair.

It is only at this point that they may become unsure and may need to be caught as they plonk their derrière onto nothing but thin air.

To those watching, the moment of magic has already been witnessed. The beauty of this exercise lies in the simplicity of its message.

If you set yourself a big enough goal then the objectives take care of themselves.

Suddenly the keys are no longer the main focus and are dealt with intuitively and with little fuss, whereas during the first attempt to retrieve the keys the objective seemed impossible.

It is the power of intuition that really comes out in this activity. Most of the big decisions in life evolve through our intuitive sense of whether it feels right or not, and it is for that reason that everyone should experience this Stanislavskian lesson once in a lifetime.

100 Who Wants to Be Out of Here?

When – End.

Why – A revision technique that allows the class to accrue points. And what do points mean ...?

Exactly. And the points in this game are converted into minutes which can then be used, literally to buy time, hence the title.

How – With roughly 15 minutes to go, announce that there is going to be a quiz (my inspiration, as if it wasn't obvious, is Chris Tarrant's *Who Wants to Be a Millionaire?*).

So with that in mind, may I suggest this as a structure you could play around with:

Q1   Should be far too easy = 5 seconds

Q2   A bit easy = 10 seconds

Q3   Easy = 20 seconds

Q4   Slightly harder = 30 seconds

Q5   Quite hard = 1 minute

Q6   Hard = 2 minutes

Q7   Getting harder = 3 minutes

Q8 Very hard = 4 minutes

Q9 Rock hard = 5 minutes

Q10 So hard even you don't know the answer = 10 minutes

Nominate a team captain whose job it is to say the final answer.

Have as much fun as you want with this game, build up the tension and maybe use a couple of the lifelines such as '50/50' or 'phone a friend'.

Maybe the class could pick a student who has to phone a parent for the answer.

I do feel that whatever the outcome of this activity, everyone may not leave the room millionaires, but will definitely be a bit richer for the experience.

101 Pass the Clap

When – Beginning, middle or end.

Why – I wanted to finish with *Pass the Clap*. If only we could all pass the clap I think that more people would be itching to have fun and expand their horizons.

This is one of the first games I ever played and is still one of the best. It is, if you like, the daddy of team games.

Energetic, competitive and team-centred, it proves that we are psycho-physical. Our minds affect our bodies and our bodies affect our minds. It also allows a lucky few the opportunity to scream out the name of a vegetable at the top of their lungs, which I believe you can include as part of your five-a-day.

How – If at all possible split the room into two teams. Place one row in front of the other.

The objective of the game is to 'pass the clap' down the line as fast as you can. To do this the first person in the team must turn to the next person and clap their own hands together, the next person does the same and the next and the next, etc. ... What you are looking for is a ripple effect – a clap, clap, clap, clap, clap, clap, clap. When the clap reaches the last person that person must raise their hands in the air and shout out the name of their favourite vegetable. My advice is to go for something short, like peas. 'Peas' is much easier and quicker to say than 'asparagus tips'.

The Rockets

Once the game has become established, and the two teams are getting competitive, you can take it up a notch or two.

To help the teams move more quickly get them all to squat, with their hands out at the ready. You will see an immediate difference in the speed and effectiveness of the teams because they are now in a position ready to take action. If they are standing with their hands in their pockets or their arms folded, then they are not ready to play.

Then the final stage is to get the entire team to shout out as much encouragement as possible to every member of their team. It is worth practising the shouting because very often people will just mumble something like 'You're the best, go on, yay'.

This is not the stuff that great teams are made of.

Get them to shout as if they have just won an Olympic gold, or the World Cup or the Lottery.

Again, the difference in speed, concentration and desire is immediately obvious. The teams will be faster, quicker, better. Not to mention that the competitive element by now will be reaching fever pitch.

So please feel free to finish the book and then promise me that you will endeavour to 'Pass the clap' within the next 48 hours.

I dare you.

Final word from the author

So there it is, I don't know about you but I'm knackered.

101 ways to start, end or break up a lesson.

I hope that you have enjoyed reading this book as much as I've enjoyed having an excuse to ignore my family for weeks on end, sipping frothy coffee and listening to classic tunes from the eighties.

Now, I feel, that seeing as I have given you 101 of my best ideas, it is only fair that you give me at least one of yours.

If there is a genius idea, technique, game or activity that you can't quite believe has not been included within this compendium of classics past and present, then please stew no longer and e-mail me at

david.keeling@independentthinking.co.uk

and I will endeavour to include it in my next book entitled *The Little Book of Other People's Ideas to Start, End or Break Up Lessons*. Catchy, eh?

If you have enjoyed my book, may I suggest you buy another copy and give it to a friend as a birthday gift or Christmas present, or just as a thank you for being such a great mate, and before we know it you'll be more popular, I'll be able to retire and everyone's a winner.

Thanks again for reading.

I love you.

Bibliography

Argos Catalogue Argos

Brearley, M. (2001) *Emotional Intelligence in the Classroom,* Carmarthen: Crown House Publishing

Curran, A. (2007) *The Little Book of Big Stuff About the Brain,* Carmarthen: Crown House Publishing

Einhorn, N. (2003) *Card Magic,* London: Southwater

Friedman, T. L. (2006) *The World is Flat,* London: Penguin

Gilbert, I. et al. (2006), *The Big Book of Independent Thinking,* Carmarthen: Crown House Publishing

Gilbert, I. (2007) *The Little Book Of Thunks®,* Carmarthen: Crown House Publishing

Wallace, D. (2006) *Yes Man,* London: Ebury Press/Random House

Index

Index

Start with Basics

Tactical Awareness

Teamwork

Whole–Brain Thinking

Wordsmanship

When?

Index

End

179